LA
217.2
.W54
1997

Chicago Public Library

SO-ANN-416

Six steps for reforming America's s

Λ Rainbow Book

SIX STEPS FOR REFORMING AMERICA'S SCHOOLS

A Guidebook for Change

– Sim O. Wilde, Ed.D. –

Library of Congress Cataloging-In-Publication Data

Wilde, Sim O., 1928-
    Six steps for reforming America's schools : a guidebook for
change / Sim O. Wilde.
            p.   cm.
    Includes bibliographical references (p.   ) and index.
    ISBN 1-56825-059-2 (alk. paper)
    1. Educational change--United States. 2. Public schools--United
States. 3. Education--Aims and objectives--United States.
4. Educational equalization--United States. 5. Education--Social
aspects--United States. I. Title.
LA217.2.W54   1997
371.01'0973--dc21   97-7404
                                                                  CIP

SIX STEPS FOR REFORMING AMERICA'S SCHOOLS
A Guidebook for Change
by Sim O. Wilde, Ed.D.

All inquiries (as well as library/retail/wholesale/distributor/STOP orders)
should be addressed to:

Rainbow Books, Inc.
P.O. Box 430
Highland City, FL 33846-0430
Editorial Offices Telephone/Fax: (941) 648-4420
Email: NAIP@aol.com
Individual Orders: (800) 356-9315, Fax (800) 242-0036

Cover quote: Benjamin R. Barber, "America Skips School." *Harper's Magazine*
Vol. 287, No. 1722 (November, 1993): p. 45.

Cover and Interior Design: Betsy Lampé

Printed in the United States of America.

DEDICATION

TO

Winifred Price Wilde, Mother and Friend,
and
Simpson Ownbey Wilde, Father and Teacher.

ALSO BY SIM WILDE . . .

Snyder's Letters, a novel

"On the Road With the Twentieth Century Luddite," an essay, and winner of the 1991 N.C. Writers' Network Creative Journalism Contest

THANKS

To my readers – Marion Blackburn, Rick Davis, Mary Lewis Deans, Harold Denton, Jim McCain, Alice Sluder, and Daisy Thorp. I made some changes they recommended, which is about all any critic can expect.

To Dr. Vance Grant at the National Center for Education Statistics for understanding my obvious shortcomings with numbers.

To the staff at Pearsall Library, North Carolina Wesleyan College, for their helpfulness and for not treating me like a freshman.

To the reference librarians at Braswell Memorial Library, Rocky Mount, NC, Brenda Greene, Alice Hildreth, Alice Niece, and Susan Reese for their indefatigable patience and courtesy.

To Erwin, my wife and best friend, for her astute criticisms and unwavering support.

CONTENTS

ACKNOWLEDGMENTS

The author and the publisher gratefully acknowledge permission to reprint excerpts from the following material:

U.S. Department of Education, *Digest of Education Statistics 1996* (Washington, DC: U.S. Government Printing Office, 1996) for extensive use of statistics.

The Commission on Skills of the American Workforce, *America's Choice: High Skills or Low Wages* (Rochester, NY: National Center on Education and the Economy, 1990), p. 45.

Margaret Mead, *Culture and Commitment* (NY: Bantam Doubleday Dell, 1970), pp. 87-88.

Benjamin R. Barber, "America Skips School" *Harper's Magazine,* Vol. 287, No. 1722 (November, 1993): p. 45 and "Index," Vol. 291, No. 1744 (September, 1995): p. 9.

Field Report from Kaolack, Senegal Field Office, PLAN International, Childreach, 155 Plan Way, Warwick, RI, Summer, 1995.

Mary Fran Spencer, "Retrain Teachers? Let's Retrain Society Instead," Raleigh (NC) *News and Observer*, (May 30, 1993), p. 25A.

Kathleen O'Leary Morgan, et. al., Editor, *State Rankings 1993*, (Lawrence, KS: Morgan Quitno Corporation, 1993), pp. 117-129.

Paul Gagnon, "What Should Children?" *The Atlantic Monthly*, Vol. 276, No. 6 (December, 1995): p. 67.

Two Associated Press releases: (1) On the first page of the sports section of the Raleigh (NC) *News Observer*, November 27, 1995, and (2) In the Rocky Mount (NC) *Telegram*, November 2, 1995.

1994-1995 National Federation Handbook, National Federation of State High School Associations, Kansas City, MO.

Robert Sinclair and Ward J. Ghory, *Reaching Marginal Students: A Primary Concern for School Renewal* (Berkeley, CA, McCutchan Publishing Corporation, 1987), p. 14.

Everett Reimer, *School is Dead* (NY, Bantam Doubleday Dell, 1971), p. 176.

Harold Hodgkinson, "American Education: the Good, the Bad, and the Task," *Phi Delta Kappan*, Vol.74, No. 8 (April, 1993): pp. 619-623.

John Herbers, "Local Govenment Needs Reinventing, Too," *The Washington Spectator*, Vol. 19, No. 20, (November 1, 1993, p. 1.

John E. Chubb and Terry Moe, *Politics, Markets, and America's*

Schools (Washington, DC, The Brookings Institution, 1990) p. 68.

School Athletics: Problems and Policies by Educational Policies Commission. copyright 1954. Washington, DC: National Education Association. (some portions paraphrased)

Ryan Whirty from a sports news story in the Rocky Mount (NC) *Telegram,* November 21, 1995.

John Hoerr, "Commentary", *Business Week,* No. 3168 (July 9, 1990) p. 45.

Lawrence A. Cremin, *Popular Education and Its Discontents* (NY, HarperCollins, 1990), p. 29.

John Holt, *The Underachieving School* (Cambridge, MA, Holt Associates, 1969), pp. 28-29.

Chester A. Finn, *We Must Take Charge: Our Schools and Our Future* (NY: Simon and Schuster, 1991), pp. 117-118.

Alan Ehrenhalt, "Learning From the Fifties", *The Wilson Quarterly,* Vol. XIX, No. 3 (Summer, 1995): p. 29.

John Rosemond, "The Best Parents Take Their Stand", from a column in the Raleigh (NC) *News and Observer,* December 19, 1995.

Public School Forum of North Carolina, Raleigh, NC, "Who Will Teach Our Children?", an undated brochure.

Nicholas LeMann, "Making It, Pt.2", (A review of *Getting In: Inside the College Admissions Process* by Bill Paul, Reading, ME, Addison-Wesley, 1995) in *The Washington Monthly*, vol. 28, No. 3 (March, 1996): p. 48.

Michele N-K Collison, "As Students Cram Rooms With Electronic Gadgetry, Colleges Scramble to Meet the Demand For Power", *The Chronicle of Higher Education*, Vol. XXXVIII (September 25, 1991): pp. A1 and A42.

Bart Giamatti quoted in Howard Cosell, *What's Wrong With Sports* (NY: Simon and Schuster, 1991), p. 37.

George H. Douglas, *Education Without Impact* (NY: Birch Lane Press, 1992), pp. 169-170.

INTRODUCTION

What must be done to reform American public education? Should we adopt a voucher system, add computers to every classroom, spend more money per child, improve teachers, their salaries, or the way they are educated, agree on more precise goals for schools, revise the curriculums, impose stricter requirements, lengthen school days and/or years?

Probably.

But there isn't any point in implementing these possibilities, no point in designing more elaborate plans, until we first take the six *more fundamental* steps set forth in this book.

Step One

Give top priority in family, community and national policies to the welfare of children.

Step Two

Establish some form of national management and funding for our educational system.

Step Three

Create an educational system that provides primarily teaching and training, not parental or community service.

Step Four

Design alternative programs for students not suited to the academic programs of the school.

Step Five

Eliminate or drastically revise compulsory school attendance laws.

Step Six

Base all progress through schools or alternative programs on performance, not just attendance.

These are good steps. They are practical, uncomplicated, and less expensive, in terms of what we get for our money, than our current obsolete malfunctioning system. We know they will work. Everything that is good about American life – parenting, teaching, and learning – tells us they will work. Everything bad about these areas tells us they are not being used. But implementing them will not be easy. Our current school system has been woven, stitch by stitch, into the social, economic, and cultural fabric of our lives. In short, our schools are what our society is, and both need fixing.

Why not change America by starting in the most logical places, where our hearts and futures are, in the schools? Isn't it possible that by changing them, we can change ourselves; and who knows how else to do that? Who knows a better way to steer us away from the violence, the greed, and the racism that divide us?

CHAPTER ONE

The System

AMERICAN PUBLIC SCHOOLS ARE the world's largest and most expensive baby-sitting agencies. Five days a week, they take in some 50 million children, transport most of them at public expense, and stuff them 25-to-30 in a classroom, often in unattractive, uncomfortable buildings, for six hours a day, 180 days a year. We pay the least possible wages to those who teach them, feed them, entertain them, monitor their behavior, and discipline them. If they need counseling, psychological appraisal, a doctor, a dentist, eye glasses, or a pair of shoes, the schools will try to supply them, providing a host of professionals with doctor's and master's degrees, teachers, administrators, counselors, psychologists, librarians, secretaries, janitors, maids, and bus drivers.

We see the results each spring in those great charades known as "Commencement," where better than 2.2 million students [1] graduate from 22,610 American high schools. [2] Grinning from ear to ear, pretending they have achieved a significant milestone, they stride across a stage to receive their diplomas amid the cheers and admiration of family and friends. They wear academic caps and gowns, the symbols of scholarship and enlightenment, but most of them are officially certified incompetents, signed, sealed, and delivered to the American people as being capable. They have the power of the vote but not the slightest idea about how to support themselves, make intelligent decisions about the nation's problems, or function as adult citizens. American public education, as we originally established it, and as we have continued to maintain it, has been a noble concept, a grand experiment to see if a democracy can endure when at least a majority of its citizens are educated well enough to make competent judgements about difficult issues, manage their own affairs, and control their political destiny.

It is what Thomas Jefferson meant in 1816 when he said, "If a nation expects to be ignorant and free, in a state of civilization, it expects what never was and never will be." [3]

It is what Calvin H. Wiley, the first state Superintendent of Common Schools in North Carolina intended when he said in 1855, " . . . and may all . . . the colleges, academies, and schools of the State be bound up in the public mind . . . as one indissoluble interest, and make common cause in behalf of one common end . . . the good of the people." [4]

It is what Lawrence Cremin in 1965 called the "genius" of American education. There is " . . . no more noble view of democracy," he wrote, "than as the dedication of society to the lifelong education of all its members." [5]

Through the years our public schools struggled with government officials who resisted educating the masses, bigots who wanted their beliefs forced into the curriculum, racists who would have shut them down, religious groups who opposed secular education, censors who would have chosen what children can know and read about, and special interests that would have used them for private purposes. Public schools absorbed the native and foreign born, rich and poor, talented and untalented, Catholic, Protestant, Jew, Arab, Caucasian, Negro, and Asian in an admirable attempt to teach the fundamentals of the English language, American democracy, and the free-enterprise system.

Even under the best of circumstances, it was a difficult assignment, and, to their everlasting credit, the schools have tried, supplying armies of trained and highly educated specialists in learning, reams of lesson plans and curriculum studies, and millions of tons of supplies and equipment. They have organized and reorganized themselves into every conceivable format, continually searching for ways to handle the burden of educating all the children of all the people. They have survived because they are the best resource most of our children have to overcome the limitations of their birthrights, the only way they can hope to have a viable future.

But in recent years, operating much as they did 100 years ago, American public schools have been overwhelmed by the problems of a technological age and by the policies we adopted to organize, direct, and finance them. In reality, they never worked as well as they should have. It was sheer romantic idealism to think that, by using the same teaching methods and the same curriculums, we could force-feed millions of children from a wide variety of economic and social backgrounds and have them come out, like sausages from a meat grinder, model American citizens. Schools became middle-class institutions, largely ignored by the rich upper class, and they routinely either denied access to nonwhites and the poor or provided them substandard opportunities.

In the 1950's, 1960's and 1970's, the American people initiated sweeping legal, social, and attitudinal changes in a number of areas. A technological revolution, that will not be reversed and will continue its inventions indefinitely, has generated a knowledge explosion and a greater need for skilled human services. We live in tense and dangerous national and international communities that struggle to adjust to the consequences of a too-soon arrival of the future. From 1950 to 2000, we will have nearly doubled the number of children to be educated [6], but we spend our resources largely for the pleasure of adults. Our legal and social systems favor the rights of the individual while our communities are fractured with severe divisions. Instead of creating a common culture, we have allowed a more diverse culture to develop, one where our differences are fast becoming greater than our similarities.

> Most employers look at the high school diploma as evidence of staying power, not of academic achievement. The vast majority of them do not even ask to see a transcript. They realized long ago that it is possible to graduate from high school in this country and still be functionally illiterate.[7]
>
> —Commission on the Skills of the American Workforce, National Center on Education and the Economy

Our mission to provide every child an equal opportunity for a good education remains valid. Our method does not. Parents and educators already know and essentially agree on what a good system of education should do, what knowledge and skills are needed to function successfully in a technological age, and what adult qualities are necessary for an economically strong and politically stable democracy. What they have not yet accepted is that the existing system of American public education cannot deliver the services needed to achieve these objectives. With great debate, furor, and political manipulations, we propose a variety of schemes to keep our public schools working, and none of those schemes will make the substantial changes our nation requires.

Our children, unequipped to deal with the modern world, deserve better, and our democratic society, whose future could very well depend on what we do about that, also deserves better. We need a new model that places children first in our families, our political priorities, and our educational systems.

As a first step toward that new model, this book identifies six fundamental problems with American education that must be addressed before any other reforms can take place, recommends six steps that can be taken to correct them, and suggests ways parents can prepare children for an educational process in the 21st Century.

What is wrong with American public education, and what can be done about it? Before those questions can be answered, the reader must first know the fundamentals about the massive nature of the enterprise: its characteristics, grand objectives, institutions, people, funding, and numbers – especially its numbers.

All societies, from simple to complex, have certain important educational objectives they consider essential for their children to achieve. The more complex the society, the more complex the knowledge and skills needed and the more complicated the educational tasks.

In a primitive society, the family assumes the primary responsibility for educating the young. The tasks are simple and taught by example. Fathers show sons the role of men and how to hunt and fish, tell stories about the history of the tribe, and teach the required civic and social obligations. Mothers teach their daughters about being a wife and mother and what it means to be a woman in their society. There is a distinct advantage to this system of education. Primitive children learn what they learn when they have to know it, that is when they use it and live it. The daily format of their lives is an educational system clearly aimed at teaching what is needed for the individual and the community to survive. What they learn is firsthand, at the heels of their parents and other adults in the community, and it is put into immediate practice. This "need to know," that is, to know something at the time it is necessary, is the strongest motivation in any learning process. It is practically nonexistent in bureaucratic education systems where children are taught what the society thinks they may need in some distant future.

> . . . I believe we are on the verge of developing a new kind of culture, one that is . . . a departure in style from (the other cultures). I call this new style pre-figurative because in this new culture it will be the child, and not the parent or grandparent, that represents what is to come. Instead of the erect white-haired elder who, in post-figurative cultures, stood for the past and the future in all their grandeur and continuity, the unborn child, already conceived but still in the womb, must become the symbol of what life will be like. [8]
>
> — Margaret Mead in *Culture and Commitment*

In a complex society, parents and the community are also a part of children's education, but requirements for survival are much more complicated and demanding. Childhood and adolescence are extended for years, so that it takes longer to become an adult. Identity problems (Who am I? Where do I fit? What am I to do with my life?) are frequent. Children have only vague ideas about their parents' work. Schools are irrelevant to the personal and professional lives of most parents, isolated places somewhere out there to send the children to "get" an education. In so doing, they surrender much of the responsibility for the most demanding and rewarding task of parenting: the teaching and training of their own young. What else can they do? Even if they wanted to do it themselves, few parents have the expertise or the time to teach their own.

So, at great expense, complex societies establish schools, staff them with professional surrogate parents, and require the children to attend in order to learn all those things biological parents can't teach but think are important. Such a process forces children into schools at artificial ages, starts them all at the same time, ready or not, and eventually dumps them out, educated or not. Practically everything children are taught is, for their purposes, irrelevant, and there is no immediate, practical application, no easy, convenient way they can implement what they are learning. Rather than education happening in an informal and natural way, required learning attempts to *make* it happen in a formal and unnatural way. The result is boredom, hostility, and resistance.

In America, our intent has been to assimilate a country of immigrants with diverse backgrounds into a common culture. The public schools were to have been an important part of that effort. They were intended for the poor, a common school for the common man, carved out of the rich man's private-school tradition but providing everyone with the knowledge necessary for a stable society. That motivation led us to develop a system with the unique characteristics listed below.

Education in America is a blend
of public, private, and proprietary agencies.

In the 1600's and 1700's, schools in America were scarce and public schools a rarity. All of them were European transplants and most were private. The idea of an education for everyone was considered unnecessary, expensive, and, in some quarters, dangerous. The word "education" did not appear in The Constitution, and even such a believer in universal education as Thomas Jefferson probably never dreamed that one day there would be massive systems of schools and colleges serving millions of students at public expense.

Since the newly organized federal government ignored education, it was left to the states to decide what might or might not be done with it. Most didn't do anything for years, relying on local private and public groups to attend to school matters. Private and proprietary schools took up the slack for governments and carried the burden for education in America well into the 1870's, when the common, or public school movement, begun in the 1830's, took hold. By 1918, all of the 48 states had passed compulsory school-attendance laws. Alaska and Hawaii would later join the Union with the same requirements, and American public education, locked into the organizational and management system it has to this day, had become big business.

The great majority of students are associated with public schools and colleges, but the legacy of private and proprietary schools remains, involving 26 percent of institutions and 12.9 percent of the people involved in American education. [9] It isn't likely this situation will change. In 1925, the United States Supreme Court established the right of parents to satisfy compulsory school attendance laws by sending their children to private schools. [10] In addition, the private enterprise system in this country will always produce schools that can make a profit and still serve an educational need.

However, this book is largely about public education, even though a blindfolded visitor placed in a classroom in either sector would be hard put to tell the difference. In general, students in private schools will be whiter, richer, and better behaved, but that could also be true of a public school in a better part of town. Any school picked at random in either sector might or might not need new buildings, better equipment, or more funding. Instructional methods are essentially the same. In the primary grades, children run about in a bustle of activities and learning groups, and in junior and senior high schools and colleges, students will be sitting and listening, textbooks open on their desks, and teachers will be standing and talking, textbooks open in their hands.

Public education in America
is a state and local government function.

It is a state function because the Constitution left it to the states, and it is a local function because the states passed on much of their responsibility to local governments. The significant factor here is that public education in America, unlike many industrialized nations of the world, is not a federal function. That is, there is no central system funded and managed by a national agency. There is no national standard, no systematic general funding and no agency empowered to hold all the states or all the local governments accountable for what they do with their systems of education.

The federal government's involvement is basically in three categories:

1. *Legal protection* in the schools of guaranteed constitutional rights such as free speech, freedom of and from religion, and equal opportunities;
2. *Research and record keeping* done largely by the U.S. Department of Education; and
3. *Minimal funding* at specific times for specific purposes Congress deems important.

Public education is universal, free, and compulsory.

It is universal and free because it is compulsory. By mandates from each of the 50 state constitutions, all children at a certain age must go to school. If everywhere children must go, then everywhere there must be a school, and everywhere it must be available at no charge. In every community in the land, regardless of distance or difficult terrain, there will be a school, a classroom, a desk, a teacher, and a means for getting children to them.

Somebody, of course, must pay for those services, but they are free to the children, and, although everyone goes, the important thing is that everyone *can* go. This one feature, free schooling, makes a policy statement of the highest order. It is a commitment from the people that education for all the children of all the people is a top priority, not only for the sake of their children but for the well-being of the nation.

> From Confucian China to Imperial England, great nations have built their success in the world upon an education of excellence. The challenge in a democracy is to find a way to maintain excellence while extending educational opportunity to everyone. [11]
>
> —Benjamin R. Barber, Walt Whitman Professor of Political Science, Rutgers University, in *Harper's Magazine*

*Public education provides
a ladder system of opportunity.*

If schools are available everywhere, there is also the option of obtaining higher levels of learning. From primary to middle grades to junior high to high school to college to graduate programs, and, even when all formal avenues have been exhausted, to continuing education and in-service courses, students can proceed through the system largely at public expense. In theory, opportunities are equal, but many students are treated unequally because of the inequities of funding from such a diversity of agencies. Moreover, not all students are equal in ability, motivation, family background, or social circumstance.

Public education is constitutionally
free of sectarian religious instruction.

Since its inception, public education has been a target of religious groups who would have sectarian religious principles in the curriculum. When Horace Mann of Massachusetts, the father of the common school idea in America, first proposed public schools for every child, some of his most bitter opponents were clergymen in the Boston area who feared an education system free of religious teachings or influence. Through the years, lawsuit after lawsuit has challenged some religious practice in the public schools: common prayers, sectarian prayers, unified prayers; a pledge of allegiance that violates religious principles; textbooks or school bus rides to children in schools sponsored by religious groups; and sectarian classes taught after, before, or during school hours, on or off school grounds with regular or special teachers.

However, freedom of and from religion is an American right that does not end at the door of a public school, and the Supreme Court, much to the consternation of many religious groups, generally takes a suspicious view of any activity that would breach the "wall of separation" between church and state.

Public education is an enormous operation.

At least 167,377 agencies run American education, providing varying degrees of direction, control, support, supervision, influence, and funding to our educational enterprise. They include state legislatures, state departments of public instruction, public elementary and secondary school districts, their boards, and their schools, private elementary and secondary schools and their boards, public and private colleges and universities and their boards, post-secondary, non-collegiate, public, private, and proprietary institutions, educational organizations and associations that service the above agencies and their professionals, and the federal government's own Department of Education. [12]

> We will pay any price for the education of our children, because our best seeds and our dearest fields are our own children.[19]
>
> — Mayassine Ka, Chief of the Village of Goria, Senegal, in a Field Report to Childreach

At least 77 million people – 30.3 percent of all Americans [13] – are directly involved in all these systems as students, teachers, staff, and board members, or they are with organizations directly involved with education. Over one-half of us from ages three to 34, 98.9 percent of us from ages seven to 13, and 96.3 percent of us from ages 14 to 17 are enrolled in some type of formal education. [14]

The cost for just the traditional avenues of education (elementary and secondary schools, and colleges and universities) in 1993-94 was a staggering $479,100,000,000. [15] In some years the expenditures for education are as much as 35 percent of local and state expenditures for all purposes and 19 percent of local, state and federal government expenditures for all purposes. [16] They can average nearly $1,821 for every man, woman, and child and

$7,151 for each elementary, secondary, and college student enrolled.[17] If diverted annually, they could pay off the principal of the February 27, 1997, national debt of $5.3 trillion in 11 years.[18] (See Appendices D and E for more detail.)

If you are having trouble understanding that kind of money, think of it this way: if you had $479.1 billion dollars, you could exchange it for 479,100,000 one-thousand-dollar bills, or, if there are such things, and if you felt light-headed enough, you could get 479,100 one-million-dollar bills for it.

CHAPTER TWO

What is Wrong With American Public Education

THE SLOWEST METHOD FOR SOLVING a problem is to create a course of study, place it in a school curriculum, and require all children to take it. A good educational process, like the mills of the gods, takes its time and grinds exceedingly fine. It is not supposed to solve problems. It prepares its students to be problem solvers. It is an interactive, not an exposure, process involving equal commitments of time and effort by students and teachers.

Public education in America is a mandatory exposure system that demands little commitment from its students and must take its share of responsibility for the many severe problems we have today: racial and social conflicts, high crime rates, loss of self-reliance, inadequate planning for the future, and a weakening of family values and structure, to mention a few.

Our system does some things well:

- It makes schools accessible everywhere to everyone, a remarkable achievement for any country.
- It provides a common social experience for most of the country's children, a circumstance that has kept our society

much more stable than it would have been otherwise.
– It takes children off the streets, off the hands of busy working parents, and temporarily keeps them out of the work force, processing them into holding patterns, until they can be graduated and moved into society at a more convenient time.
– It teaches many children what they need to know, especially if they are white, prosperous, and middle class.

These services have been, and continue to be, valuable to our local and national communities. There are good public schools, and many children profit from them. But, too many children receive an inadequate education, or they are not being properly challenged. Why? What is wrong with American public education? This chapter discusses six fundamental problems that must be addressed, and the flaws they create corrected, before other reforms can be accomplished.

The welfare of children is not a priority in families, community, and national policy.

We live in a period of swift and continuing change that Margaret Mead called a "pre-figurative" culture, that is, a culture where only the children know what it is like to be raised in their time. [1] That is in stark contrast to a "post-figurative" culture where change is nonexistent, or at least much slower, and where children grow up in traditions and beliefs similar to their parents. Technology is a primary cause of our rapid change. Today, through technological machines and with little censure, we invite the world into our homes. These machines dominate our lives, teaching lessons unheard of in previous generations and overturning stable and enduring values. New ethical conflicts confront us daily. Guidelines parents learned from their parents are considered obsolete. Even the roles of children, parents, grandparents, and the growing number of stepparents, are complicated and confusing. Add to all this the busy schedules of working parents, the growing number of single parents who must leave children unattended, and the creation of lifestyles for the pleasure and benefit of adults, and we have a culture hostile to the proper care and nurture of children.

The dismal statistics confirm that over the past four decades the circumstance of children in America has worsened:

– Sixteen percent of white children, 41 percent of Hispanic children, and 43 percent of black children live in poverty.[3]
– America's infant death rate ranks 22nd among industrialized nations, and our child mortality rate is 19th.[4]
– Child abuse cases in 1991 were 29 percent higher than in 1985. Although sexual abuse is offensive enough and gets more attention from the media, of the 2.7 million reported incidents of child abuse (some experts say many more go unreported), three-fourths are for neglect and physical abuse. [5]

> The problem of children unable or unwilling to learn, and the resulting chaos, is a problem spawned by our society and the economy that drives it. It is poverty and poor health care, nutrition, and parenting. It is alcohol, crack, broken homes, crumbling family structure, no moral training, child neglect and abuse, and gangs. It is living in the midst of random violence in a world which children can't understand or change. Making it racial is too easy. Making it the world we have created is too painful. [2]
>
> —Mary Fran Spencer, Retired Teacher, Wake County (Raleigh, NC) in the Raleigh *News and Observer*

– The youth suicide rate has tripled in the past 45 years. [6]
– In 1990, 67 percent of births by adolescent mothers were to unmarried women, up 15 percent from 1960. [7] Forty-eight percent of births by single women in 1992 were to those who did not complete high school, up from 35.2 percent in 1982. [8]

For too many children, home and community environments are not conducive to healthy mental, emotional, and physical development.

– The one million divorces in this country annually, involving a million children, are an increase of 68 percent from 1950. [9]
– Since 1970, the number of children under 18 with a single parent has more than doubled from eight percent to 18 percent. [10]
– Of all poor children, 46.4 percent of Hispanic, 49 percent of white, and 85.5 percent of black live with a single parent. [11]
– In 32 years, the rate of working, married women with children under six years old increased from 19 percent to 60 percent.[12]

Children are much more likely to be poor than senior citizens, and the federal government will spend much more on the elderly than it will on children. That is not likely to change since the elderly have money, political influence, and ever-growing numbers. The Age Wave Institute tells us that two-thirds of all the men and women who ever lived to be 65 years old are living today, and the Population Reference Bureau says that, by 2025, the elderly will outnumber teenagers by more than two to one.[13]

Educational opportunity is unequal throughout the country,
and the national responsibility for education is disjointed.

Think of American public education as if you were the chief
executive officer of a big business that provides educational services to its clients. Your company has a corner on 88 percent of
the national student enrollment market, kindergarten through
grade 12, because clients (students) are required to use the kinds
of services you provide, and you propose to do anything for any
of them, no matter how physically, mentally, or emotionally ill-
equipped they may be. Furthermore, your services are cheap,
and the only other option is a private school, which is more
expensive, not always available, and, as a rule, not willing to
take just any client.

Since your company requires no performance standards for
its clients, there is no need to provide quality services. But clients are bored, unmotivated, and unruly, and many of them,
when the law allows it, quit in frustration and disgust. Staff morale is understandably low. Money is tight, and, although prices
should be raised, it is more and more difficult for you to explain
how costs have multiplied in recent years with no significant
improvement in services.

As a chief executive officer, you know you must quickly
convince your board of directors that if the company is to survive, radical changes must be made in its organizational and
management style. The problem is you have thousands of boards
to convince, not just one, and there are also thousands of chief
executive officers with just as much authority as you. Turf wars
are daily occurrences in the tricky political climate among federal, state, and local governments, their school districts, and their
individual schools. None of them would agree that you can speak
for them, and none of them feels responsible to you or to any

other educational agency.

In the past 75 years, we have become a nation with strong national goals and a citizenry highly dependent on a centralized federal government that regulates most of its important functions. At the same time, we have developed a highly independent and individualistic school system, administered by 50 different states with over 14,772 politically entrenched local school districts which manage more than 85,393 schools. In policy, finance, management and organizational structure, there is no national accountability, no coordinated leadership, and no external performance standards for schools or students. Since everybody's business is nobody's business, public education is a management disaster.

Unequal educational opportunities in America are caused mostly by inconsistent inadequate financing and enforcement of standards. How do you answer the following questions about public education in America? How much money is spent on children's education, and what are the sources of funds? How many students are each of their teachers assigned, and how many administrators and supervisors does it take to oversee and direct them? What are the minimum and average salaries of teachers? How many and what kinds of courses must high school seniors complete for graduation? How many days a year must schools be open, how many minutes per class, and how many hours in a school day? At what age are children required to attend school, and how well is the law enforced? Are students required to take minimum competency tests before graduation? Are their teachers required to take them to be certified?

The answers to these and other questions about American education are that it all depends on the state, city, county, or street address of a child in question. The funding of education in this country, like its management, is fractured by thousands of agencies, and the quality of education available is an accident of birth. From state to state, from school district to school district, and within districts from school to school, there are wide discrepancies, "savage inequalities" [14] Jonathan Kozol calls them, in per capita and per pupil expenditures for education. Money alone will not give us a quality educational program, but a modern quality educational program requires money, and every child in it deserves equal funding.

Most of the money for public elementary and secondary schools comes from state and local governments which share the burden equally. Nationwide, local governments average paying 41.7 percent of the costs, state governments average 41.7 percent, the federal government 16.7 percent. [15]

As of 1993, the educational funding systems in 14 states have been found unconstitutional, and in 18 other states they were being challenged. [16] Why? Consider some recent examples of unequal school funding practices among the 50 states and the District of Columbia (see Figure 1, the next page).

> We used to say — and too many educators will say — that we cannot compare our schools with those of other countries because they educate only an elite, and we try to educate everybody. Untrue for thirty years, this is now the opposite of the truth. They educate the many, and we the few. To our shame, a disadvantaged child has a better chance for an equal and rigorous education, and whatever advancement it may bring, in Paris or Copenhagen than in one of our big cities. [19]
>
> —Paul Gagnon, Senior Research Associate, Boston University, in *The Atlantic Monthly*

Figure 1
Recent Examples of Unequal School Funding Practices

Among the states [17]

Per capita expenditures for education by state and local governments in 1991:

Highest	Alaska	$2,285.59
Lowest	Tennessee	918.72
National Average		1,227.97

Expenditures for education as a percent of all state and local government expenditures in 1991:

Highest	Indiana	37.34%
Lowest	Alaska	20.47%
National Average		29.11%

Per pupil expenditures for public elementary and secondary schools in 1992:

Highest	New Jersey	$8,793
Lowest	Utah	2,827
National Average		5,097

Average teachers' salaries in 1991-92:

Highest	Connecticut	$48,900
Lowest	South Dakota	23,927
National Average		35,905

Figure 1, *continued*
Recent Examples of Unequal School Funding Practices

Among the states [17], continued

Graduation rate in public high schools in 1990:

Highest	Vermont	91.65%
Lowest	Louisiana	56.67%
National Average		71.20%

Number of pupils per teacher in 1992:

Lowest	Vermont	13.5
Highest	Utah	25.3
National Average		17.2

Within the state boundaries

*The differences in expenditures, per pupil, for schools (1989-90) between the richest and poorest districts [18]:

Alaska	$13,040
Massachusetts	$ 7,058
New York	$ 6,286

Public schools try to correct all of society's problems, provide every ser-
vice every child needs, and teach everything every child should know.

Our founding fathers created a democracy based on what
they called "self-evident truths." Foremost among them was the
idea that "all men are created equal." What that means is that all
people in America, male or female, of any race, creed or color,
are born with certain basic political rights that should provide
the protection of life and liberty. They are not born with social
or economic rights or the right to inherent talents, and their right
to happiness is the equal opportunity to pursue it, not have it.

However, we have designed an educational system that attempts to make everybody "equal" by giving one and all the
same kind of education: the mentally, physically, and emotionally handicapped, the normal and abnormal, the smart and the
not so smart. But our society has grown more diverse, has placed
the good of the individual over the good of the community, and
has created private wealth and public debt. The resulting demands on the schools have been overwhelming as they have
struggled to make the melting-pot concept a reality.

The real truth of it is that from our genes to our environments, from the womb to the grave, there has never been equality in human affairs. On the contrary, the world's people, though
similar in many respects, have been created with remarkable
diversities. Given their birth circumstances, all individuals in all
cultures must achieve for themselves whatever levels of success
they can, must accept the concept expressed by Ralph Waldo
Emerson, that the only significant achievement an individual
makes is through hard work within the limitations of his own
circumstance and talent.

Children are not equal, and they cannot, to any degree of
success, be made equal. Too many American people think they

can be. They make their schools responsible for everything children need, including those responsibilities normally reserved for parents, and then they place all the children in those schools, regardless of skills, talents, backgrounds, intelligence, or maturity and give them all essentially the same kind of educational experience.

It is necessary in a democratic society to think of all citizens as important and to apply all laws fairly to everyone, regardless of race, creed, gender, or station in life. All people must be given the same means to pursue happiness according to their own naturally endowed talents, cultural differences, and levels of effort. Equality is not the goal. Equality of opportunity is.

Furthermore, American public schools fracture their efforts by assuming too many responsibilities only minimally related to learning. They have expanded their functions to include all the needs of their students not met by their families: food, clothing, medical and dental care, social and athletic activities, and psychological support and treatment. If they had dormitories they would be, like hospitals and prisons, total-care institutions.

Studies show again and again that teachers and students spend inordinate amounts of time daily in off-task classroom duties unrelated to learning such as record keeping, discipline, health, welfare, and personal needs, bus duty, hall duty, and lunchroom duty. The worst and most widespread practice is engaging teachers and students in selling almost anything imaginable (candy, turkeys, pizza, magazines) to pay for almost anything imaginable (band uniforms, library drapes, toilet paper, cheerleader travel expenses, athletic equipment). T books written on the subject with titles such as " for Your Children's Schools." They should be t Use Children to Hustle the Public."

Educators defend the proliferation of their

by arguing that a student who is hungry, ill, or disturbed cannot learn, and so his or her needs must be attended first. Exactly. The personal needs are met, the educational needs are not, and the schools have become expensive, inefficient day-care centers.

Athletics provide the best example of how we have allowed an extracurricular activity to dominate our educational system. Thousand of players, coaches, cheerleaders, sports writers and booster clubs, 845 national sports organizations, millions of adoring fans, and a number of television networks will attest to the cult-like devotion America has for athletics. It has become a national obsession, a "secular religion," [20] and even the most unenthusiastic fan knows that America's real heroes are athletes.

Nobody knows for sure how many organized teams there are at all levels of competition in the 40-plus sports we play, how many players compete, how many people attend the games or watch on television, what the gate receipts are, or what the value is of all their franchises, stadiums, courts, fields, and equipment.

An excessive involvement in athletics in a society empha-

> Charles Haley comes across as the meanest man on the Dallas Cowboys. Teammate Nate Newton may be one of the jolliest guys in all of football. Exact opposites in positions as well as personality, both agree the Cowboys (10-2) must be more Haley-like for Dallas to win the NFC East title, lock up home field advantage for the playoffs, and keep everyone healthy. "We've got to find a killer instinct," Newton said. "We've got to start nailing people to the ground. We've just got to start crushing people." [21]
>
> — Associated Press release in the Raleigh, NC *News and Observer*

sizes masculine traits, aggression, and violence. Coaches train their players as if they were going to war, send their troops into battle, and pace along the sidelines, anger and hatred in their faces as they rage at the officials. Players speak of the love of hitting others and of giving more pain than they get. Strutting like gamecocks, they openly taunt their opponents while delighted fans roar approval. Sports writers use the brutal language of a violent society playing its violent games: crushed, stung, clobbered, slammed, hurt, smashed, blocked, muscled, and rocked. Communities tolerate the criminal celebration antics of fans who regularly vandalize goalposts, buildings, and city streets after games.

Nowhere are athletics more entrenched than in American education whose institutions consider them as much a part of the educational process as English, biology, or history. What started as an inexpensive, recreational diversion for students on Saturday afternoon or an occasional evening has become a major parasitic industry, using our educational system to fulfill parental fantasies, entertain the public, publicize schools and colleges, and make money. From the little leagues to the professional teams, highly organized, intense, varsity athletics send a clear message to our children that what is important is the athlete, not the student, that what matters is the game, not the learning. Sports advocates argue that athletics make a significant contribution to education. Their main suppositions are: they are fun, they teach valuable lessons, they keep students in school, they make money for schools and colleges, and they build community spirit and pride. Are they right? Yes and no.

Sporting events are "fun and games" for spectators. For players, parents, and coaches, they are serious business. Playing any kind of athletic game is fun. Being on a varsity team or any of the little league teams means intense hard work and fierce contests with the ultimate aim being anything but recreation. Students can learn valuable lessons from participation in varsity athletics: the development of mentally and physically disciplined bodies, proper diet, avoidance of alcohol, tobacco, and drugs, performance under pressure, cooperative skills needed for good teamwork, and so on. But these lessons are learned only by the varsity few, not by at least 80 per cent of the other students, most of whom do not even have active, viable intramural athletics offered to them.

Some students do remain in colleges and high schools because of athletics. In colleges, although graduation rates are often poor, varsity athletes stay for very substantial motivational reasons. In the first place, they are paid to attend. In the second place, for most sports, college enrollment is the only option for those who want to continue their training as professional athletes. In the third place, most hope someday to be a part of that small percentage selected for professional teams.

Students in 17 states and the District of Columbia are already required to stay in school until age 17 or 18, and, in the rest of the states until age 16. [22] Furthermore, since the "dumb jock" image is a myth, it is likely that better than 90 percent of the estimated 3,170,305 boys and girls who participated in 1994 in the 10 most popular high school sports (See Appendix I) functioned adequately as students. They would have stayed in school and graduated, with or without athletics. The remaining 10 percent (317,030) represent 2.1 percent of all high school enrollment and an average of 14.4 students per high school. [23] Can we justify the enormous amounts of time, energy, and money we spend on athletics to retain a small percentage of students whose only interest is in an extracurricular activity?

In high schools, with rare exceptions, athletics do not earn their expenses. Activity budgets, including athletics, are usually an estimated one to three per cent of total school budgets, and are one of the first to be cut in financial hard times. Athletics directors, hard pressed to pick up the shortfall, increasingly turn to private and business support. High schools in some areas are placing business logos on team uniforms, hanging company banners in gymnasiums, and giving companies free tickets to athletics events and space in sports programs. Some entrepreneurs are showing interest in televising state championship games. Television already controls the tempo and the schedules in college athletics. It is only a matter of time before we have national high school bowl games or high school coaches, like their counterparts in higher education, endorsing shoes, clothing, and soft drinks. In March, 1996, *The Virginian-Pilot* (Norfolk) reported that a former high school star at a Norfolk high school said that "gamblers routinely approached players last season about fixing games." [24]

Varsity athletics build community and school spirit for winners but not for the majority of teams that have mediocre or losing seasons. Communities or states which must rely on their sports teams to boost their morale expect their coaches and players to win, and, if they don't, their losses are often considered personal failures reflecting on the integrity of the entire community.

There are no satisfactory alternatives to school.

Americans think education is a place, not a process, and that school plus attendance plus 13 years equals education. They think this way because, for 100 years, schools and their schedules have been so tightly woven into American society that parents accept packing the children off to school in the mornings as a necessary function of family life. School schedules make life comfortable for parents. They can go about their own affairs secure in the knowledge that their children are safely stored away *in loco parentis*, in the place of the parents, under the care of legally responsible professionals. The children, their attendance mandated, have no options, no matter how poorly the school serves their needs.

All children should be in school some of the time, some children should be in school most of the time, and some children should continue through graduate school. Schools should be academic centers, that is, institutions where formal studies are conducted about what the society thinks is important for its children to know. Schools do not and should not be expected to function efficiently as anything else. They may incidentally provide athletic, entertainment, medical or social services, may serve caretaking functions, but the extent to which they do detracts from their primary purpose. The one criterion for remaining in school, at any stage of development, should be that students can demonstrate they have the potential to continue formal academic studies. When students have accomplished all they can in a school, for whatever reasons, laziness, poor background, emotional immaturity, lack of intelligence, or inappropriate programs, they should be released or transferred to alternative programs better suited to their needs: work, day care, apprenticeship, home studies, or any other avenue appropriate to their individual circumstances.

The problem is there are no alternatives. The public schooling process, give or take a few curriculum options, is the same for all students, offering essentially the same kind of instruction everywhere. School systems like to think otherwise. They say they teach by the principles of individualized instruction, that teachers determine the needs of each child and then apply methods suitable for meeting them. That's what parents expect, what colleges train their teachers by, and how supervisors evaluate teachers' performances.

But teaching children one on one in public schools where there are wide differences in backgrounds and abilities is impossible. Public education in America is a system for the masses. One can hardly expect individualized instruction when 50 million students each year are herded into crowded elementary schools where teachers are responsible for all subjects all day every day for 25 to 30 children or into junior and senior high schools where teachers have 100 to 150 students a day shuttled in and out of their classrooms for 50-minute periods. Teachers could effectively teach by individualized methods if students not suited to academic programs could be transferred to alternative programs.

School curriculums are oriented toward the academic, as they should be. This requires proficiency in the language arts, but those who do not read, write, speak, or listen well do not perform well in schools, and, in fact, get progressively worse as they move through the system. Some of these will quit when the law allows, lacking in all but rudimentary skills and unemployable except for menial jobs. The rest will wait out a few more unproductive years and graduate, still not proficient in the language arts and still unprepared for work. Our society appoints these students to the status of second- and third-class citizens because they failed or rejected a school program they found unbearably dull and irrelevant to their needs. The most

> . . . most schools tolerate the existence of a fringe population that is not fully involved in the mainstream of school life. These marginal students learn and contribute only a fraction of what they can and thus use only a portion of their potential at school. [25]
>
> —Robert L. Sinclair and Ward J. Ghoryin in *Reaching Marginal Students: A Primary Concern for School Renewal*

critical task of an educational system is to teach each individual the means for economic self-sufficiency and the self-respect and sense of accomplishment that go with it. That should be at the top of anybody's educational priorities, well above the sciences, the liberal arts, American history, or physical education.

Compulsory school attendance laws gridlock the system.

In all 50 states, compulsory school attendance laws require children somewhere between the ages of five and 18 to go to some school. In most states they are not required to graduate, and there is no common standard of performance except exposure for a certain number of years. Grades, achievement levels, and diplomas are meaningless since progress through the system depends largely on simply being present at school, regardless of how useless or inappropriate that may be.

Although there are notable exceptions, most states tend to define school attendance, more or less, as a requirement for a child to attend a building that has been declared a school that has 36 weeks of five six-hour days, during which pupils are under the supervision of teachers who engage students in educational activities.

Over the years, school attendance laws have been rigidly enforced by some states and ignored by others. At times some states abolished their laws and their public school systems in failed attempts to avoid racial integration, but the courts have rarely tolerated challenges, confirming again and again the right of states to have school attendance laws, indeed declaring that, since they exist for the common good of the society, they override the natural rights of parents. The U.S. Supreme Court has made two notable amendments to the laws: allowing children to satisfy requirements at private and parochial schools, and, because of their unique religious background, excusing Amish children, regardless of age, after they complete the eighth grade. [26]

Supporters of these laws argue that there is essential information in any society that all citizens must know if there is to be any semblance of a common culture. Left to the immediate interests of children or the whims of parents, these essentials for a stable society might never be learned. Education in a democracy, they say, is too important to be left to the discretion of individuals.

Critics have responded that neither culture nor education can be made to happen, that schools where attendance is required are not concerned with education but with discipline and control, that schools are no longer the sole source of information they once were for students, and that bureaucratic school systems dominate the lives of children, isolate parents from the education of their young, and contribute to a weakening of the family unit. They argue that if schools are made attractive, relevant places of learning and if parents are left to assume the responsibility for the education of their children, compulsory laws will be unnecessary.

But compulsory school attendance laws, with the weight of the legal system and public opinion solidly behind them, remain the stickiest of the glues holding our public education systems together, and that seems agreeable to most parents. Americans are terrified at the thoughts of being responsible for their own children 24 hours a day or of the possibility of millions of other people's children swarming daily through the streets because they don't have to go to school. Children ought to be in school, society says, and parents agree – even if the children hate it, even if it's the wrong place for them to be, even if they're not learning anything. And everybody should be there, we seem to think: the lame, the halt, and the blind, the geniuses, the average, and the retarded, the undisciplined, the emotionally disturbed, and the violent.

When attendance is a requirement, not a privilege, the school's energies are directed not at learning but at controlling behavior. Parents assume it is not their responsibility, but the government's, to educate their children. The children do not see education as a reciprocal, interactive process. On the contrary, they assume that the right to an education means a guarantee to *have* it, and that you get it by attending a school or a college and having something done to you, like an x-ray, a haircut, or a blood transfusion.

> Institutional monopoly of education, especially by the state, has all the evils of a state church.... The school, in modern times, has become more powerful than the church of the middle ages. The career and, therefore, the life of the individual depend upon his success in school. The law makes him a criminal if he does not attend it. He is subject to its influence far more than medieval man was ever subject to the church. The case for a prohibition of educational monopoly is stronger than the case against a state church.[27]
>
> —Everett Reimer in *School Is Dead*

Progress throughout the system is based on attendance – not on performance.

Each year, thousands of students graduate from American high schools with diplomas that mean little more than 13 years of attendance. Few of them have experienced the valuable learning that comes from a critical and demanding evaluation of their performances. On the contrary, unacceptable levels of achievement are routinely given passing marks, especially when students faithfully attend classes. Rewarding a poor performance devastates potential for future quality. Giving good marks for mediocre or poor work misinforms students and parents, and, worse, destroys incentive. Eventually, all of us, teachers, students, and parents, lose sight of what a good educational performance is.

Graduates know that official compulsory education has left most of them with few competencies for employment, little or no understanding of the world and how it operates, and no knowledge of the disciplined effort required for excellence in a work area. Public education's basic concept, "the whole child," is concerned with the overall development of children, socially, emotionally, and academically. Under this idea, students are considered better off when they are "socially promoted," that is, when they are passed along through the system for the sake of overall development even if they have not mastered previous academic performance levels. If a student's overall academic achievement is far below a given level, he or she will be moved into more difficult levels anyway in order to avoid a failure stigma or being separated from current classmates or the wrath of parents. Even though good students get good marks and pass on to higher levels of learning, their potential is not fully challenged. The average students, who are rarely motivated, and the poor students, who are lost, watch their incompetencies stack higher and higher each year. Negative attitudes toward the learning process become firmly entrenched. The majority, once they have quit or graduated, will never again participate in a formal educational program, in spite of the increasing demands of a technological age.

CHAPTER THREE

How We Correct What is Wrong

WHAT MUST WE DO TO CORRECT THE problems of American public education? The answers are far less complicated and far less
expensive than most of us think.

*Families, communities, and national policies
must find ways to give top priority to our children.*

A democratic educational system does not operate in a
vacuum. Its quality is directly related to the quality of the homes
that produce its students. No matter how we design it, children
cannot be educated or trained when they are undisciplined,
emotionally disturbed, ill, or disadvantaged. Parenting, especially
in a democratic society, must be considered an honorable, lifelong commitment not only for the well-being of the children but
also for the nation.

To that end, our society must help parents develop a lifestyle
that complements an educational experience for the children.
There must be some tangible rewards for being good parents,

and there must be penalties, perhaps even forfeiture of parental rights, for those who place children in jeopardy. Both father and mother may be working or a single parent may be struggling alone to make ends meet. They may be busy and tired and have their own interests to pursue. But everything they ever wanted for themselves, their children, or the country at large will be in vain if those children grow up ignorant, unemployable, and undisciplined.

> ... if we were told that an unfriendly foreign power had disabled one-third of our youth, rendering them incapable of reasonable performance in school, we would view it as an act of war. We don't need to imagine a foreign enemy; by systematically neglecting the needs and potential of disadvantaged children, we have done the damage to ourselves. [1]
>
> —Harold Hodgkinson, Director, Center for Demographic Policy in *Phi Delta Kappan*

There is a direct correlation between an individual's standard of living and the quality of his or her education. Because of our shameful history of oppression, discrimination, and neglect, we have created a financially dependent group of people, largely nonwhite minorities. This underclass grows larger by the year and has the potential for making our society much less than we have always envisioned it. Unless that problem is addressed, for every child who gets a good education, there will be another who is a rapist, a killer, or a drug addict, and millions of dollars worth of additional prisons won't hold them and won't solve the problems.

There are three primary responsibilities parents must accept for the education of their children. They must:

1. Provide a home and community environment that is conducive to learning and places the needs of the children first in family priorities;
2. Take responsibility for fundamental parental duties such as teaching respect for authority, developing mature emotional habits, and encouraging principles of human decency and consideration for the social welfare of others; and
3. Participate in the educational process not only in support of children but in continuing their own education.

The point has already been made that Americans have more and more shifted parental responsibilities to the schools, but the schools are a poor substitute for a mother or father. Parents are the only ones who can perform parental duties well. The dilemma is that if they do not, the schools cannot perform their duties well, either. We should encourage whatever policies we need for the establishment of quality homes and schools, and we should provide communities which provide quality childhood environments – but unsatisfactory results occur when either one attempts to assume the duties of another.

*America must establish some form of national
management and funding of its educational system.*

At the time of this writing, the image of the federal government is in disrepute, and popular sentiment is that much of its control and regulatory power should be given to the states. Maybe the federal government should be more decentralized or the states given more control. Maybe all governments should give less attention to the regulation of their citizens' personal lives. But, if the federal government is unmanageable, *that* is where corrections should be made. John Herbers, former *New York Times* national correspondent covering state and local government, said, " . . . most Americans do not appreciate the enormous size and importance of the state and local government sector in the life and economy of the nation and what a large bite it is taking out of the economy without sufficient return in services." [2] Dumping critically important responsibilities on state and local governments is not the answer. In a world of technology, international threats and domestic problems confront the entire nation, not the individual states.

> . . . America's institutions of democratic control are . . . significant obstacles to the improvement of its schools . . . if the nation wants better schools, it will need to govern them through very different institutions than it has in the past. [3]
>
> — John E. Chubb and Terry M. Moe in *Politics, Markets, and America's Schools*

It is no more logical for the states to have their own educational systems than it is for them to have their own postal or defense systems. If America is to remain a strong and viable nation, it must have a clear-cut *national* mandate for quality educational opportunities for all its children, and only the federal government has the authority and the resources to do it. That means national policies, standards, testing of student performances, and finances. It also means reorganization so that some national authority, either Congress or an independent agency it would create, could bring consistency and accountability to American education.

Education costs a lot of money whether we pay for it privately or publicly. But in a democracy, the education of our children is an absolute necessity, a national priority, an investment that must be skimmed off the top of our income. Currently, we spend disproportionately more money on too many other areas of American life than we do on education. Unless our priorities are rearranged and our inequalities in funding corrected, government of, by, and for the people will become the government of fools and ignoramuses.

We must create an educational system that provides primarily teaching and training, not parental or community services.

As long as the American society thinks its schools can correct all its ills, as long as we expect schools to make unequal children equal, to make silk purses out of everybody's sows' ears, the results will be as inevitable as they are with any system that tries to be all things for all people. Nobody is served well.

Democratic education is a collaboration, an equally shared obligation among groups and agencies and each with its own unique responsibilities. The government must offer quality educational opportunities for all children who choose to take advantage of them. The educational system must teach. Parents must provide basic emotional and physical needs. Communities must maintain a safe and supportive environment. Each one does what it can do best and is always accountable to the others, but in no circumstance should one group take over the responsibilities of another. The failure of parents, for example, to fulfill their obligations is not a reason for the educational system to assume them.

Our public schools currently have too many activities which distract teachers and students from their main purposes. Those extraneous activities are there because our society, including the state, parents, and local communities, dump too many of their responsibilities onto the schools. Here are some of the operating principles schools should implement. Practicing teachers could add dozens to the list.

- Parents must prepare their children for a classroom setting. Those too undisciplined, immature, disruptive, or violent to participate in a group learning process should be sent home.
- Severely handicapped students, physically, emotionally, or mentally, should be in mainstream classes only when they can perform at the same levels as other students.
- Students, staff, or school resources should not be used to raise funds for any reason.
- School staff should be able to make referrals to appropriate agencies, but should not attempt to provide welfare or social services such as food and psychological and medical treatment. Obviously, lunches must be available but not as a free service and should possibly be catered by private business.
- Teachers' time must not be used for a host of clerical and monitoring duties not directly related to student learning.
- Parent associations or athletic booster clubs should not use school staff and/or facilities to accomplish their own agendas.
- Schools should de-emphasize athletic programs. In 1954, the Educational Policies Commission, a distinguished body of American citizens appointed by the National Education Association, published *School Athletics, Problems and Policies*. This slim little book outlined some of the false values and bad practices that marred athletics in too many high schools of the day. American educators should have read it more closely.

Figure 2, with some elaboration, accounts for what has happened in 43 years – what they say occurs "when a high school student body attaches false values to the importance of interscholastic athletics." [4]

Figure 2
The Results of a High School Student Body
Attaching False Values to the Importance
of Interscholastic Athletics

1. When the school, the community, the players, and the coaches are convinced they must win, the school program is frequently disrupted, and, under the guise of school spirit, athletics replace educational priorities.

2. Home team athletes are excessively pampered, glorified heroes who receive privileged treatment from the educational program and the community at large, and opposing team athletes are hated rivals to be humiliated or injured.

3. Referees and umpires are targets of derision, and games are played as public spectacles where wildly partisan spectators, many of whom have no connection with any school, are unruly and unsportsmanlike.

4. Schools recognize and promote participation by a few varsity athletes and neglect the many who would participate in intramural sports or other types of competitive recreational activities.

5. Parents are obsessed with athletics, expecting their children at an early age to compete among highly organized, pressure packed community teams, creating such inanities as elementary school all star soccer teams that travel from city to city and Pee Wee football leagues that have a final national "super bowl" championship played by 10 and 11-year-olds.

6. Coaches are expected to compromise integrity, if necessary, to produce a winning team, and, as long as they win, their tactics and their influence on the attitudes and character development of their players is rarely questioned.

If all that sounds familiar, it is because 40 years later those false values and bad practices, and more, have become worse. Athletics staged as gladiator-like events, with cheerleaders and bands and screaming spectators have little educational value. They may generate enthusiasm for the schools, provide recreation for the players, and entertain students and the public in general. But those purposes are not what high schools are about. In fact, they lead the list of extraneous activities detracting from the overall results we need from our educational process. Watching athletic events does not educate our children, make them more knowledgeable citizens, teach them how to become responsible adults, or provide the skills to support themselves and their families. A small number of varsity players and a smaller percentage of superstars may benefit, may even become millionaires, as a result of their participation, but the educational programs of the vast majority suffer for it. High schools were not established to provide, at public expense, training camps and farm teams for collegiate and professional athletics.

> Tarboro (NC) High School football coach, Bruce McFerrin, was asked to resign after a two year won/lost record of 9-11 because his team did not make post-season playoffs. Co-athletic Director Don Reams said: "He's a good man, and he did a lot of good things. He's had a rough two years. He really tried hard to help our young people." Principal Lana Vanderlinden said: "I wish he could have won more games at Tarboro. He's a wonderful coach and a man of great integrity. He is a role model in the classroom and at Tarboro High. I hate to lose someone the students have so much respect for." [5]
>
> —Ryan Whirty in *The Rocky Mount* (NC) *Telegram*

None of this means that there is no value in varsity athletics, in the physical training programs involving them, in the lessons to be learned from group cooperation and teamwork, or, from the spectators' point of view, in watching exciting sports events. But it does mean that education can never be taken seriously in America and reforms can never be implemented as long as our high schools, colleges, and universities place the emphasis they do on athletics or as long as they are known more for the quality of their athletic teams than for the quality of their educational programs.

An educational program should ask one question of any activity it sponsors, whether it is a task performed by a teacher or administrator, a student function, or a community activity affiliated with the school: does it contribute to our priorities of teaching, training, or learning? If it does not, it should be revised, de-emphasized, or eliminated.

We must design alternative programs for students not suited to the academic programs of the school.

Ultimately, the most important achievements for all children are to be emotionally and financially independent, able to leave home and make it, find a job and keep it, and support themselves and their families. For these reasons, an educational process, whether it is professional, technical, or vocational, should be realistically tied to the world of work. Children should know from the beginning that their learning is oriented toward that which will give them the greatest sense of pride, accomplishment, and self respect: an employment best suited to their talents and levels of effort.

These opportunities will only be available when American

public education designs alternative educational programs which will provide more options than the single, traditional, expensive-for-what-we-get, obsolete blender we now call a school. Some of our children, by the accidents of birth and upbringing, are intellectually oriented for the academic learning schools can provide and should be given maximum opportunities to benefit from it. Some children are not, and, except for the most fundamental lessons of a common knowledge, should be given options more suitable to their needs. Some of us can be philosophers and some of us surgeons and some of us truck drivers. All are important to a society.

Consider first the role of the school. All children should begin their formal education in a school, and all schools should be academically oriented. Assume that for the first nine years, from what is now kindergarten through what is now the eighth grade, or until students are about 14 years old, the school would have three purposes. The first purpose would be to teach the attitudes necessary to be students, making four points very clear:

> High school graduation this June was the beginning of adulthood for 2.6 million young Americans who received diplomas. But for 40% of this group, the million-plus graduates who will not go on to college, it will be like stepping into a black hole. Most of them face a period of prolonged unemployment or low-paying, often part-time jobs. The reason: there is no link between school and work in the United States. [6]
>
> —John Hoerr in *Business Week*

1. Getting an education is their responsibility;
2. The entire educational process will be aimed toward making

them independent and economically productive citizens of their communities;

3. Their participation will demand discipline and good work habits; and

4. Respect for the authority structures, traditions, human rights, and ethical obligations of our society are paramount if an education is to be of any value.

The second purpose would be to teach the fundamental body of facts, skills, and understandings necessary to function effectively in the American society. It will not be difficult to determine the content of this "shared knowledge" since most educators and parents already agree as to what it is: fundamental English language skills, the basics of arithmetic and science, a knowledge of the rich American heritage and how our nation came to be what it is, an understanding of the Constitution and its democratic values, and an appreciation of the arts.

The third purpose would be to assess students' cultural backgrounds, intelligence, performance, and capabilities in order to make decisions about the educational directions each should take when elementary school is completed.

Throughout the elementary school years, the school will have periodic discussions with students and parents about students' strengths, weaknesses, and capabilities. The objective of these assessments is that by the end of the ninth year, everyone will be clear about what the best option is: to continue on in school or to transfer into an alternative program.

Those qualified to continue in school may choose an alternative program, but if they remain in school, they will be preparing for higher education studies, whether they plan to go to college or not. They will continue their studies in the essential body of shared knowledge until graduation, with more rigor and intensity and with an emphasis on applying critical thought about what they are learning.

Even with periodic evaluations of student progress through the elementary school, there is certain to be some disagreement at the end of the ninth year about where a student is to be placed. It will be critical to the success of alternative programs that the school have the final say in this decision, but it need not be a permanent one. Those remaining in high school who cannot or will not meet its more demanding performance requirements will be allowed to shift into an alternative program. Students placed in alternative programs who present evidence of their capabilities or a change in attitude may be allowed to transfer back to the school's general studies. Parents would have the option they have now of withdrawing a child for attendance at a private school, or they might choose an alternative of their own.

> The (public education) system needs to be re-connected with the life of society. Young people need to have a greater range of opportunities to pursue their interests and to do so in real situations in association with working adults who are not kin. More mature people need to have a greater range of opportunities to pursue their vocational and avocational interests in a variety of institutions that are accessible, welcoming, and ready to tailor education to individual needs and backgrounds. [7]
>
> —Lawrence A. Cremin in *Popular Education and Its Discontents*

If we abolish compulsory school attendance laws, as recommended later, children of any age must voluntarily choose to participate in the educational options available to them, and completing the requirements of a school or alternative program must be in terms of performance, not attendance, also recommended later.

Consider next the role of alternative programs, which also are already well-known to educators and parents. For years many high schools, in cooperation with community businesses and professional offices, have offered distributive and vocational education programs for students who attended traditional school courses for part of the day, and, under school supervision, worked part of the day.

Alternative programs would expand on that idea. Defined, they are non-school activities which match students' cultural backgrounds, intelligence, abilities, and interests with experiences, either in education, training, or work, which will contribute to their overall development and lead to productive employment. In short, students after the age of 14, who do not function well in a school, would spend 30-35 hours weekly in work-related activities in their communities which are better suited to their abilities and interests.

A number of categories of these activities would benefit alternative program students.

— Internships in day-care centers, nursing homes, hospitals, schools, libraries, art galleries, and museums for those interested in becoming full-time workers in those areas;
— Part-time workers in a wide variety of jobs: landscaping, greenhouses, yard work, construction work, fast foods, grocery stores, stock and inventory clerks, car washes, freight depots, house painting, or a host of others;
— Clerical and/or secretarial work in professional and business offices: using keyboards for typewriters or computers, collating, copying, stapling, mailing.

- Apprentices in a variety of skilled crafts such as wood working, machine shop, automobile repair, and printing or in the
  creative arts such as painting, pottery, and acting;
- Assignments to self-employed parents who are farmers, store
  owners, plumbers, electricians, or heating and air condition-
  ing mechanics;
- Miscellaneous individual assignments to homes to keep house,
  care for preschool children or brothers and sisters for a single
  parent or both parents who work, and, with qualified parents,
  home-school studies.

These activities will require changes in child labor laws
which aim to keep children restricted in what they can do or
attempt to keep them out of work altogether. The intent here is
to make alternative programs legitimate, supervised educational
or training activities. They would be based at the schools, and
students enrolled in them would have the same social and athletic privileges, subject to their work schedules, as any other student. The programs would be administered by facilitators who
would locate activities and match them with students' interests,
performance records, and teacher recommendations. Students
would meet regularly with other Alternative Program students
and take courses in "jobology": the art and science of getting a
job and keeping it. They could be paid after a trial period if they
proved themselves worth it. They would be evaluated, as any
other employee, by on-the-job supervisors, including the possibility they might be promoted or dismissed.

These ideas will lead the American people through un-
charted territory. Acceptance of alternatives to school will require concerted political maneuvering and skilled organizational
talent, largely because of old, established myths about children
and youth: that they should be in school no matter how inap-

propriate, that they should be carefree and without responsibilities, that it is unhealthy for them to work even for a few hours a day, and that they can't be socialized unless they are in school.

On the other hand, the possibilities are unlimited for creating alternatives for students adrift in schools not relevant to their life circumstances. Allowing them to participate and accepting their satisfactory completion of an alternative program as worthy of a diploma would immeasurably improve the quality of their lives as well as the quality of the schools they leave.

Eliminate or drastically revise compulsory school attendance laws.

Since it must be acquired, and cannot be imposed, the only worthwhile education is a self-education. Forced learning is a form of indoctrination and eventually serves neither the student nor the enforcer. Chil-

We should abolish compulsory school attendance. At the very least, we should modify it, perhaps by giving children every year a large number — 50 or 60 — of authorized absences. Our compulsory school attendance laws once served a humane and useful purpose. They protected children's rights to some schooling, against those adults who would otherwise have denied it to them in order to exploit their labor, in farm, shop, store, mine, or factory. Today the laws help nobody, not the schools, not the teachers, not the children. To keep kids in school who would rather not be there costs the schools an enormous amount of time and trouble, to say nothing of what it costs to repair the damage that these angry and resentful prisoners do whenever they get the chance. [8]

—John Holt in *The Underachieving School*

dren must be taught that, even with support from parents and the community, and even if the state provides a free, quality educational opportunity, they are responsible for their own learning.

That is a lesson they will never learn unless compulsory school attendance laws are abolished or radically altered to give educational institutions – whether they are schools or alternative programs – control over their social and academic circumstances. No institution can maintain its credibility and integrity when it cannot control who participates and who does not or who stays and under what conditions once they are involved.

If we could survive the necessary political struggles to abolish school attendance laws in, say, North Carolina, what would the likely impact be on their million or more public school students? On one day the laws are in effect, and the children must be in school. On the next day the laws are gone, and they don't have to be there. What would happen? Would there be any drastic changes? Would some parents allow state legislatures and the local counties and cities to stop funding education? Would some children revolt against their parents, refuse to participate, and joyfully run screaming through the streets? Would some parents sigh with relief, take the children out of school and put them to work? And if they were too young for work, would some parents let them stay home all day and watch television? Would some working parents agree that one of them would have to stay at home during the day, or, at least pay someone else to stay for them?

Some or all of that would probably happen but not enough to bring about significant changes in attendance patterns. Couples who can afford for one parent to stay at home, and working parents who must have a place to park their children, will continue to insist on the best possible public education at public expense. The poor and disadvantaged, wherever possible, will daily continue to send their children to meet the school buses, even if the educational system is bad because that is still the best possible hope for their future.

The rest, the parents who will not or cannot provide the family and home support necessary for their children's education, may allow them to drop out of the system, but that won't matter. Those parents don't give adequate support now, and their children, uncomfortable for the most part in the academic setting of the school, are already out of the system, either physically dropping out when the law allows or dropping out in spirit, bored and disruptive, as they dismally wait for graduation.

When it becomes clear, after several years of basic general education and assessment of their potential, that they should not be in an academic setting, they will profit from a transfer to alternative programs better suited to their needs. They will be better off and so will the schools.

Imagine this scenario the first day students return to school without being required to be there. When they arrive, they are called into an assembly where a principal makes remarks that sound something like this:

> You are here today not because your state has required it, but because you and your parents made a conscious, deliberate decision for you to come. You are welcome. We want you here, but your continued presence is more a privilege than it is a right.
>
> For several months your teachers have been studying ways they can teach you to be the directors of your own learning, and one night this week they will also meet with your parents to suggest how they can better support you in getting your own education.
>
> We cannot give you an education, but we can, with

your support and cooperation, help you obtain it for
yourself. We will do all we can, we will offer as many
opportunities for learning as our resources provide, but
the choice to be educated, and the responsibility for it,
must be yours. If you do not take this task seriously, if
you disrupt the learning process of others, if you misbe-
have, commit illegal acts, or refuse to put forth an effort,
we will suspend you from school and return you to your
parents until you can correct your attitude or behavior.

Every child in America must have an equal opportunity for
an education that lies with voluntary participation in quality programs and resources, not with mandatory school attendance.

*Base all progress through schools or alternative
programs on performance, not just attendance.*

Nobody works for nothing. Individuals may desire money,
compliments, recognition, approval, a good feeling, personal
satisfaction, or a combination of all, but everybody expects something for their efforts or they lose their motivations to continue.
All humans need to achieve. Achievement, that is, success in a
project, increases the desire for even higher achievement. Lack
of achievement, that is, failure, decreases the desire for higher
achievement. The simple truth of it is that success tends to lead
to further success, and failure tends to lead to further failure.

Most American families are not implementing these basic
motivational principles, have no consistent systems in place, and
present few challenges to perform well. The result is a lack of a
sense of achievement and a corresponding alienation and loss of
identity. Children can't help parents whose work is so far re-

moved from the home. There are no apprenticeships, no skills to be learned at a parent's elbow, not even a workplace to sweep out. What few household chores they are assigned, emptying garbage, washing dishes, and mowing the grass, may be aesthetically desirable for a well-ordered home but add little substance to the basic food-clothing-shelter welfare of their families.

Children and youth have no knowledge about family finances or the efforts required to supply them, and yet, without resources, they are still the targets of relentless advertising. Their only recourse is to coerce, blackmail, beg from, or wheedle adults, and to assume such activities are legitimate. In an age of technology and specialization, children are takers, not givers, liabilities, not assets.

Attending school, the business of children and youth in America, is no better, offering little worthwhile work. Most students find that schools are dull, irrelevant, and unchallenging

> The single most potent boost that could be given to student learning in the United States in the 1990's would be for all our colleges and universities . . . to inform the schools that they intend to go out of the business of remedial . . . education and that, beginning on a specific future date, none will enroll any applicant who does not possess at least (certain) skills and knowledge . . . (and if) the nation's major public and private employers were to behave similarly: deliver themselves of a solemn and sincere pledge not to hire anyone who cannot demonstrate certain skills and knowledge." [9]
>
> —Chester E. Finn, Jr., Professor of Education and Public Policy, Vanderbilt University, in *We Must Take Charge: Our Schools and Our Future*

and welcome any opportunity, sickness, truancy, holidays, or drop-out, to escape them. Those who work hard, perform well, learn what they are supposed to learn, and do what their teachers tell them, will graduate. And those who don't? If they attend, they also graduate.

The most effective motivation for students is a positively oriented educational experience with a tangible reward for achievement. An educational system should be structured so that the opportunities for legitimate success are maximized and the chances for failure are minimized. However, progress through that system, from kindergarten through graduate school, including alternative programs, must be on rigidly enforced, competency-based standards of performance. Students must be able to do it and prove it. They must know that their diplomas or certificates were earned, that they had to do more to get them than attend classes, and that their accomplishments, achieved in this manner, are far more valuable to them and to the society that recognizes them.

CHAPTER FOUR

Preparing Children for an Educational Process

PARENTING HAS ALWAYS BEEN A demanding, expensive, stressful task, but in a time of rapid social and technological change, the task becomes increasingly more difficult. Mothers and fathers once held much tighter control, frequently monitoring the location, behavior, and even the thinking processes of their children. Parents alone decided what was right and wrong, no matter what others were saying or doing and, no matter how much the children protested, set the ground rules. A number of factors have contributed to the erosion of that control.

Changing values encouraged the development
of a permissive adult society.

Changing attitudes about traditional values, especially concerning sex, race, and the role of women, were already evident in the 1950's and moved swiftly from the 1960's to the present. Those who question these changes usually blame the radical youth of the day, but they could not have been sustained without the endorsement of adults. It was adults who approved, or at least tolerated, a revolution in behavior patterns and created a permissive society in which they prosper while the children suffer.

Such a society has difficulty providing the conditions children need for healthy development: the stability of a family structure with discipline and tough love. Permissive parents *give* their children freedom thereby denying them the necessary skill of *earning* it. Such children rarely appreciate their freedoms, are slow to leave home and exercise them, and, once they do leave, have greater difficulties becoming independent adults. Such children expect adulthood to be an extension of childhood fantasies, a fulfillment of their dreams: a world that gives them everything they want with little effort and no accountability. Children do not need more freedom and more influence on family policies. What they need, and what permissive parents and a permissive society cannot give them, is a sense of being loved enough to be directed until they are able to direct themselves.

Mothers joined the labor force.

Another factor adding to the instability of the family has been the movement of so many mothers, for economic or personal fulfillment reasons, from homes to the labor force, leaving children on their own much of the time or in the care of surrogate parents. It is not necessarily a problem to have both parents working, and the last thing children or husbands need is an unhappy, unfulfilled, dissatisfied mother and wife. Problems do occur, however, in homes where members of the family routinely scatter in different directions, and working parents do not make the necessary adjustments for the proper care and development of their children. Consider the frantic lifestyles of parents in the l990's. We see them on weekdays, especially the mothers, scurrying about in the mornings, harried and hustling, juggling the schedules of homes, spouses, children, car pools, and jobs. Exceeding the speed limits, riding the bumpers of cars ahead, they rush impatiently to get the children to school or day care early so they can make it to work on time. Since arrangements must be made for the time difference between the end of the school day and the work day, children often go home to empty houses or to sitters or remain in after school programs. A sick child, holidays, teacher work days, or summers are a problem for everybody's schedules and a disaster for the single parent.

After work, the pace continues in reverse. Collecting the cargo distributed earlier, parents must stop at the grocery store, the pharmacy, the cleaners, the bank, or complete one of a dozen other errands. At last, they dash home, only to leave again for little league baseball-basketball-soccer-football practice or to ballet-piano-horseback riding classes. Somewhere in all this, between taking to and picking up from, they prepare dinner, maybe several times to serve the different schedules, clean up the kitchen,

> This generation will come to adulthood in the early years of the next century with an entirely different set of childhood and adolescent memories from the ones their parents absorbed. They will remember being bombarded with choices, and the ideology of choice as a good in itself; living in transient neighborhoods and broken and recombinant families in which no arrangement could be treated as permanent; having parents who feared to impose rules because rules might stifle their freedom and individuality. [1]
>
> —Alan Ehrenhalt, Executive Editor, *Governing* magazine in *The Wilson Quarterly*

supervise homework and baths, get the children to bed, collapse on the couch, doze, and finally stagger off to bed. The next morning, and the next, they begin again in the rat race that won't end until the children leave, or grow old at home.

Technology has brought rapid unending change.

Expanded communication systems are open windows into our homes, inviting the greed, language, and violence from the streets and offering our children, often in empty, unsupervised houses, as targets for national advertising.

Perhaps the most pervasive influence of a technological society has been its promotion of rapid change that leaves generations with little time to establish their own traditions. Rootlessness and the loss of personal identity with a place and a group are the only traditions of too many of our citizens. Each scientific advancement, each new machine, rides roughshod over the present and accelerates us toward a future unlike any most of us have envisioned. In spite of the pleas of some who yearn for the more simplistic values of another time, there is no turning back. The technological process is irreversible. It can only bring "future shock," confronting our children with issues for which there is no experience, no precedent, no guideline. How do parents prepare for that? How can they establish family stability and maintain control of their children in a fast moving technological society? How can parents and grandparents teach their children and grandchildren to learn from their experiences while shedding obsolete ideas? How do they educate them to become responsible adults who can bring new ideas to a world of new problems without abandoning those that have proved themselves in the tests of time?

Obviously, parents need help. One place they should expect to find it is their public education system. But, for reasons discussed in previous chapters, the current system is not serving our children and youth as well as it should. Assuming its faults are corrected, what obligations would a good educational system owe parents in assisting them with the rearing of their children? And, what obligations would parents owe the educational system?

WHAT WE WANT

In short, what should we want and not want our public education system to be, and what do we want it to do for children who will live in the 21st Century.

1. To assume it cannot correct all the ills of the American society, restricts its programs to education and training, holds students responsible for their own education, insists that parents and local communities be full partners in the educational process and that they create family lifestyles complementary to the education of their children;
2. To offer quality educational opportunities to everyone, where none are required to participate, and all are accepted for what they are and encouraged to be better;
3. To relate all its programs, vocational or professional, to practical, future employment;
4. To provide schools which are academically oriented, teach the fundamentals of shared knowledge and skills needed to function in the American society, and assist students in making wise career choices;
5. To offer, at an appropriate time, alternative programs for

those students who will not benefit from further schooling;

6. To create a setting committed to the highest standards of learning where achievement in all its programs is based on performance and competency and where learning is motivated by challenging and relevant lessons;

7. To be managed by an independent, national body that sets consistent policies and priorities for the 50 states, provides equal opportunities for the education of all the nation's children, regardless of color, creed, or ethnic origin, and designs a system on the cutting edge with the finest in equipment, supplies, and technology; and

8. To provide a positive, caring environment for learning that also demands responsible behavior: Rude, discourteous, or violent behavior would not be tolerated, and students at any age who cannot control themselves or adjust to an educational process would be suspended or ultimately expelled.

Parents have a more significant role and a greater responsibility in educating and training their children than the schools do. No school can adequately educate or train children whose parents have not performed their duties. What do we want good parents to be and what do we want them to do?

Emphasize their roles as parents and role models.

Good parenting in a technological society is not something that comes naturally. It is serious business, it has to be learned, and it goes far beyond merely supplying the young with food, clothing, and shelter. Good parenting requires the unselfish devotion of adults to the needs of the children. It requires constant attention to making children feel wanted and important and to teaching them that parents must have the same respect. When faced with the decision to be a parent to a child or a friend to a child, it means choosing to be a parent. It is coming to understand that the ability to say "No," and say it often is one of the distinguishing characteristics of a good parent, that the primary goal is to help develop children into independent, self-supporting adults who can get out of the house as quickly as possible, and that, in the end, good parents can be judged by what kind of grandchildren they have.

Create a nurturing, stable, and structured home environment.

Adults are more likely to be responsible when they come from homes where love, security, and structure are a certainty. In such homes, the pace is less frantic, individual children are expected to yield to the needs of the group, meals are regular and on time, parents are in place and participating in family activities, bedtime is early, understood, and accepted. These conditions are undoubtedly more difficult to establish and maintain in poor homes, but they can be accomplished. There is no denying that money is important to rearing children. Homes with money have children who are healthier, smarter, and better adjusted, socially and emotionally. The more money a family has, the more education the

> I believe children need parents who are self-confident to make unilateral decisions and follow through with them in the face of the most histrionic objections from their children. I believe it is healthy for children to frequently feel their parents are mean and unfair. I believe the more objection a child has to a parent's decision, the more likely it is the decision is a good one. [2]
>
> —John Rosemond from a column in the Raleigh (NC) *News and Observer*

children will get, and the more education the children get, the more money they will earn in a lifetime. But material items alone will not buy a good child. On the contrary, with toys, spending money, and clothes, less is usually better. The key factors to family stability are not money and not freedom but unity of purpose, schedule, and routine.

Attend to their marriages or to themselves, if single parents.

A home should be oriented to the needs of children, but they should be taught from the beginning that adults also have needs. Homes are stronger and more stable when parents have a satisfied marriage and/or self-respect and fulfillment as persons.

Teach children responsibility through principles of good discipline and order.

Children are legitimate, full-fledged members of the family with a right to be there no matter how much they complicate the budget or adult lifestyles. Beyond that, additional rights must be earned, and, until they are, children must obey. They need to be needed, need an identity that goes with having something around the house to do that makes a difference. From an early age they should be expected to make regular, tangible contributions to the family through part-time jobs, chores, good behavior, or good school efforts or performance, be responsible for the consequences of their own actions, and pay or suffer for their mistakes. Good behavior, that is, behavior the family wants, should be rewarded. Bad behavior, that is, behavior the family does not want, should cause privileges and favors to be withheld.

Teach children three realistic attitudes of life.

1. *People are not equal.* Everywhere, anytime, someone is smarter, dumber, richer, poorer, prettier, or uglier. The poor are disadvantaged, and the handicapped are restricted. Nothing we can do will change that. But that is not important. The key to what one wants to be or to improving shortcomings is in what one does with what one has.
2. *Life is not fair.* What one gets from it is proportionate to how hard one works and how lucky one is. Nobody has yet adequately explained why the good suffer and the wicked prosper. That's the way it is. The best preparation against an unfair life is to expect it, plan for it, and work hard to overcome it when it happens.
3. *Individuals are basically responsible for their own lives.* We expect parents to start us off with a minimum level of support and others to respect those rights the Constitution has guaranteed. Beyond that, everything must be earned, and nobody, not the government, school, or society owes us anything. That which is undeserved, without being earned, usually proves to be of little value. The only valuable help is self help. There may be rare times when we can save a drowning man or give bread to a starving child, but, eventually, if people can't help themselves, they can't be helped.

Be committed to education.

Children cannot be expected to take their education seriously when parents themselves are uneducated and show no interest in improving that situation, when a home environment discourages study and encourages unlimited television viewing,

and when the children are not required to take education seriously. Parents can show their commitment in three separate ways.
First, they can encourage positive attitudes toward education by
a firm support of the educational system and the children's involvement in it and by participating in continuing educational
activities of their own. Next, they can create a home environment that provides stability, structure, a quiet place to study,
and an atmosphere of learning that goes beyond a television set.
And, finally, they can make achievement in educational programs a part of a child's obligations to the family.

WHAT WE DON'T WANT

What we do not want in American public education could
be as important as what we want. What is it the system cannot
do well or should not do at all?

1. We must not continue the concept that education is a holding
    pattern. The education and training of our children and youth
    is lengthy, demanding, expensive, complicated and critical
    to the well-being of the nation. It is a process, not a place to
    park the children to be socialized or entertained, and it is
    not a time span such as a twelve-year lock step that everyone
    must endure.

2. We should not spend any more money or energy on any
    proposal that attempts to make the system work. American
    education in a technological age needs radical, fundamental
    change, not patchwork programs which try to make the cur-
    rent system work. Some of the proposals being suggested
    around the country are:

Freedom of choice of schools.

The idea here is that if parents could choose where to send their children, inside or outside their local school districts, the schools would be competitive and, thereby, better. But competition is the fuel of business, suggesting the drive for profit, a goal difficult to relate to educational aims. The funding and management of educational programs should be on a business-like basis, but imagine what it would mean to turn them over to free enterprise: schools designing their curriculums to meet popular demand, advertising that hawks alternative programs on billboards, radio, and television, pricing wars, and faculty violating ethical and quality standards to keep a "losing" school afloat.

The biggest problem, however, with freedom of choice is that many parents don't have anywhere to send their children other than the most convenient school, the one closest to home, and a school bus system that would accommodate any massive rearrangement of enrollment would be an expensive administrative nightmare. And it still would not address the central issue of quality. Those who can afford it will live in better neighborhoods and go to schools which are better because of where they are. Those who live in poor neighborhoods, not having much choice, will go to schools which are poor because of where they are. Nothing has changed.

Greater parental control or involvement.

Parents are not doing well now with one of society's greatest problems: the establishment and maintenance of a home environment that complements the education of their children.

They should be more involved with their children's education but as parents, not teachers.

Numerous programs to keep youth in school.

Our schools spend time, energy, and money coercing and enticing students to stay in programs under conditions and circumstances no sane adult would tolerate. We withhold drivers' licenses, and, adding insult to injury, expand the requirements for already unsuitable programs: extending the school day and year and increasing the compulsory age. We won't even let them out when we suspend them, holing them up in a classroom in an insidious practice called in-school suspension. The logic behind all these measures is that it is the students' fault if their schools do not work for them. Neil Postman and Charles Weingartner once compared this idea with doctors who say their patients die because they are bad patients. [3] Such solutions do not provide needed alternatives. On the contrary, in attempting to make the schools work, they manipulate the circumstances of the students, requiring them to take more of the same old inappropriate education, only take it longer and under more stressful conditions.

Pay teachers more and/or strengthen certification requirements.

Some teachers are, of course, inept, but requirements to improve them assume it is their fault our schools are not better. It is not. Prospective teachers currently spend up to one-half their college teacher education programs in courses that attempt to teach what can't be taught in a classroom: how to relate to and teach children. In all 50 states, teachers achieve certification by proving they are prepared for the stifling environments of mandatory public schools which have no alternatives, little motivation for students to learn, and no real performance standards. Intern teachers are always shocked at the difference between the methods they are taught to use and the methods they can realistically implement in a public school. We do need knowledgeable, challenging, exciting teachers, and they should be paid more, but strengthening current certification requirements without changes in the system will not help. What teachers need more than money or additional training is an environment that doesn't burn them out early in their careers, that makes teaching an enjoyable and rewarding experience, and that allows them to have more personal relationships with students.

> Numerous studies have found that expanded job opportunities for women and minorities, an increasingly negative public perception of teaching as a career option, low salaries, and poor working conditions are combining to make the search for excellent teachers more and more difficult . . . the most talented teachers are those most likely to leave within their first few years of teaching . . . those scoring in the top 10 percent of the National Teachers' Examination leave teaching within seven years; of those scoring in the bottom 10 percent, two-thirds remain. [4]
>
> —The Public School Forum of NC

3. We should not incorporate prayer or any form of religious education in public school programs. Religion has been, and is, important to the American people. All our children should study its historical impact as well as its current influence in the world. But

religious belief is a very private and personal matter, usually cultivated through the years by tradition, family, and worship centers. Children who don't get their religious foundation there won't get it with symbolic rote prayers or required religion courses.

Government in a democratic society and all its agencies, including the schools, is a public, community-oriented matter. It protects the freedom to be or not to be religious, but it must remain neutral to sectarian beliefs and activities. Public school cannot become a theological battle ground where various groups compete for the minds or souls of children. Rather, the two must coexist, together but separate, even if their relationship is often uneasy and troublesome.

This does not mean that our educational system, its schools and its alternative programs, cannot be moral or teach moral principles. The system should be a model of integrity that stands for good discipline and order, enlightenment, erudition, and responsibility. Everything it is and does should teach students respect for themselves, other people, and the environment, and these characteristics may or may not be tied to a belief in a supreme being. Those who argue otherwise, who want prayer in schools, who want the public to pay for teaching their particular religious ideology, who denounce an education without religion as evil, are more interested in the welfare of their religions than they are in the welfare of our children.

4. We should not allow corporal punishment anywhere, at any level, in public education. There is no valid reason for the use of corporal punishment by schools or parents unless we believe it is good policy to humiliate children or good therapy for an adult who needs to beat up on them. It is legalized

child abuse, and it becomes an art when one can administer a slap, a kick, a spanking, or a whipping without letting too much blood, breaking bones, or leaving unsightly bruises. Some schools still administer corporal punishment, but they are sexist about it, rarely spanking or whipping girls.

Corporal punishment is not an effective means of discipline, even if it stops undesirable behavior. It models violence as the solution to a problem, sending a clear message that when one has size or authority, one can treat people as one pleases. Physical violence is demeaning to the giver and the receiver, and like any other form of abuse or assault, it passes along from one generation to the other, leaving long-term effects that can cause even more rebellious behavior.

Good discipline is not a reaction to a random act. It is a training system designed to teach the kind of behavior desired. Punishment has a minor role in discipline, but in no circumstance is physical aggression against a child necessary or desirable. A good system of discipline requires care, time, effort and consistency. It is a necessary ingredient in any family setting for adults as well as children. But it doesn't just happen. It has to be planned, implemented, and monitored constantly.

CHAPTER FIVE

Enrolling Children in College

THIS BOOK IS PRIMARILY ABOUT American public elementary and secondary education, but it would be remiss not to provide some information and make some recommendations about important educational programs available to our children after high school graduation.

At last count, there were 10,426 post-secondary institutions of education in America [1] offering a variety of programs in colleges and universities, vocational and technical schools and colleges, and other types of training institutions. With only a little persistence, any parent can get any child who is a high school graduate, regardless of qualifications, into most of them.

He or she doesn't have to be a particularly bright or industrious child, may be dull and lazy, read at the sixth-grade level, have difficulty writing a coherent paragraph or turning a fraction into a percentage, and not be able to find the District of Columbia on a map or even know what it is. It doesn't matter because post-secondary education is a buyer's market. Some vocational school, college, or university, somewhere, will take even the most limited student.

The process of selecting the best college for a child to attend should be a cooperative one between parents and children. This section, however, is written primarily for parents who believe that:

1. They have a right to approve where a child should attend if they are to be partially or fully responsible for moral, physical, or financial support;
2. That it is important for a child in college to be motivated by ideas, challenged intellectually, and held responsible for satisfactory work; and
3. They will direct or assist with the college-search process.

The advice given here is designed to cut through the hype and glitter thrown up by the usual college recruiting practices and get at more appropriate information concerning the quality and integrity of their academic programs. There is no need for parents to read further if they think it is solely the children's privilege to select a college, or if they really don't care where children go as long as they graduate.

Six thousand five hundred and fifty-eight, or 64%, of post-secondary institutions are classified as non-collegiate [2] because their primary mission usually is not to provide a broad, general education but to train students in specific skills such as hair styling, truck driving, wood working or flying. Some are publicly supported, and some are private, nonprofits, but the majority, or 74%, are proprietary, that is, they operate as businesses – for a profit. Parents and children would do well to explore the possibilities offered by these more vocationally oriented schools. Their programs serve many students better than colleges or universities, and, for many, they provide better avenues to productive and rewarding careers.

If the decision is made not to attend a non-collegiate school, children can still gain admission into one of the 3,688 two- or four-year, private or public colleges or universities around the country. [3] This section will address attendance at one of those institutions of higher education because that's where American high school graduates think the action is. Colleges and universities have the appearance of a life of leisure. The high school image of partying another four years in a fun place like a college is a welcome contrast to the serious nature of learning a trade and going to work in a couple of years. Collegiate institutions have the allure and the prestige as well as 94% of the post-secondary enrollment. [4] They also have the athletic teams, the fraternities and sororities, the free time, and less than a demanding workload.

> In comparison to other countries, what's remarkable about the United States is how easy it is to get into a good college and how little where you went to college matters in the long run. [7]
>
> —Nicholas Lemann reviewing Bill Paul, "Getting In: Inside the College Admissions Process" printed in *The Washington Monthly*

Their differences are as great as their numbers in size, purpose, curriculum content, sponsorship, cost, and quality. Fifty-five percent of them are private or proprietary, [5] but the public colleges and universities enroll 78% of the students. There are extremely large institutions (28 of them, or less than 2% of the total, average 38,144 students), and there are extremely small institutions (377, or 10.5% of the total, have less than 200 students). Enrollment in all institutions averages 4,009, but 73% of all students are in institutions with 5,000 or more. [6]

Determining the differences between colleges and universities can often be confusing. Some colleges offer a four-year course of study, leading to a bachelor's degree in, for example, the arts or the sciences, which includes a heavier concentration in one subject area called a major. Universities also offer four-year degree programs, but, in addition, they will offer graduate studies which emphasize research and lead to master's and doctor's degrees. Some will offer only one or two graduate programs while others will have dozens.

Universities usually have collections of "colleges," such as the College of Arts and Sciences or the College of Medicine, but some universities will call these colleges "schools," such as the School of Education or the School of Journalism. The truth of it is that an educational institution can and will call itself whatever it wants. In addition to the 3,688 colleges and universities, most all of which are accredited by some agency, there are self-study degree programs offered by "colleges" with no campus, extension branches offering courses for students who never see their home campuses until graduation day, and fake "universities" which will award any degree desired if the price is right.

Nearly 40% of all institutions of higher education, with nearly 39% of the enrollment, are junior, community, or technical colleges which offer two-year courses of study. [8] Usually, they have programs leading to Associate of Arts or Sciences degrees, and they also offer certificate programs which may take less than two years. Many of these colleges offer general education courses with up to two years being transferable to some four-year colleges. Their tuition is usually a bargain, averaging $4,253 less than all four-year colleges, and public two-year colleges average $5,794 less than private ones. [9]

Americans have always held institutions of higher education in better regard than they have their other schools. Parents who monitor their children closely in elementary and secondary schools, observing teachers, guarding what is to be studied, censoring books, or evaluating the company of friends, will then unceremoniously drop their children at some college with hardly a thought about the qualifications of the faculty, the content of the curriculum, the kinds of students who attend, or the standards of behavior required. Where is the mother who quarrels with a college professor about his teaching methods or the father who questions a dean of women about social rules?

College graduates never think of the good old days of the fourth grade but about the beach weekends, the parties, and the escapades of college years. They remember the sarcastic, eccentric old prof who taught English Lit rather than the stern but sweet old thing who taught English in the eighth grade. There are occasional high school reunions, but has anybody ever heard of an elementary alumni association? Those who have been to college periodically return to campus, walk about the buildings, look at old dorm rooms, visit with former professors, but rarely think of the elementary and secondary school teachers who made it possible for them to be there. Few public school systems provide school teachers with the benefits and privileges college faculty take for granted: a lifetime career with, at most, a 20-hour on-the-job work week, three months of paid vacation, and, for all practical purposes, a tenure with the academic freedom to be what one wants to be or say what one thinks. No senior high school tolerates the equivalent of a drunken fraternity party brawl on campus, and no apartment house tolerates the daily misdeeds of college dormitory residents.

Why do we have such reverence for higher education? Probably because the collegiate experience is not universal and not free. Everybody had to go to elementary and secondary school, usually with no tuition and very little out-of-pocket expense. On the other hand, at one time, only a handful went or even thought about going to college and, for most families, it meant a considerable outlay of funds. This suggested an aura about colleges and universities that labeled them as special places. They were our fountains of learning, the sources of our wisdom, and the seats of our knowledge. We hired the best and most learned of our teachers, sent them the brightest, most capable of our students, and gave them freedoms we would never allow in the lower schools.

That image has changed as more and more of us, capable or not, are being accepted into colleges and universities. Competition for students is intense. All but the most exclusive institutions will do anything to get them and keep them – except to lower tuition. They hire expensive consultants to design complex admissions marketing strategies and send handsome, recent graduates with tales of football games and exciting student activities to recruit bored high school juniors and seniors. They bring prospective students on campus to see the luxurious party suites they have built in their residence halls. They overlook both poor levels of language skills and high school performances, accepting students whose credentials are far lower than their published standards. They create courses and majors the mentally impaired can pass and each year award far too many diplomas with honors. They have assumed the same policies that have destroyed the effec-

> No longer seen as a place only to study and sleep, today's dorm room must do triple duty as a living room, bedroom, and study space. "The rooms must offer the comforts of home, but must be better than home," says Dave Bartlett, a junior at Virginia Tech, who lives in a triple that he and his room mates have dubbed The Tower of Power. "It must be a party place." [10]
>
> —Michele N-K Collison in *The Chronicle of Higher Education*

tiveness of public high schools: that everybody can and should attend college, that colleges can correct whatever flaws their students have, and that attendance, not performance, is what is important in getting an education.

Students mean money. They add millions to local economies. They bring in cash each term to pay for their tuition. They buy supplies, books, clothes and food. They pay for fees, housing, and a variety of other services. They account for the all important full-time equivalency (FTE) that combines the full and part-time enrollment used by legislatures and other agencies to fund colleges and universities. A healthy, increasing student enrollment is a public relations plum which institutions use to say to the world that they are exciting, viable, fun places to be. (See Appendix F for information about where higher education gets its funding.)

College directors of admissions are under as much pressure to recruit students as athletic coaches are to win games. Administrators can work miracles in educational reform, double the number of books in the library, and improve the quality of the faculty and the instructional program, but their boards of trustees, their own peers, and the general public will judge them in terms of how much the institution "grew," that is, how much the student body increased under their direction.

Colleges and universities in America have many more problems than lowered admissions standards and the subsequent loss of quality in instructional programs. The criticisms are everywhere – in books, magazines, journals, and speeches, by reporters and writers outside the institutions and by those who manage and teach in them: the growing influence of athletics and government and corporate research on institutional policies, the lack of continuity between high schools and colleges, the increasing costs of a college education with no evidence of greater services or that students learn more, and so on.

But these problems are beyond the reach of parents and children. It is enough of a challenge to find the institution with the right fit as well as the money to pay for it. Their only option is to play the game, to use the system for whatever advantages it can offer. And there are hundreds of options. Not everyone, of course, can gain admission to any college. But he or she can get in *somewhere*. No later than the junior year in high school, a serious prospective college student and parents should be involved in three tasks:

1. a critical and honest assessment of the reasons for attending,
2. a careful search for those colleges which best fit those reasons, and
3. selection of the best college with the best price.

Let's address those tasks.

Number 1: Assessment of Reasons for Attending College.

It is often said that people attend college, not to be better educated or more informed, but to be able to get a "good" job, a nice house, and a new car so they can have an easier, more prosperous life. It is more complicated than that, of course. High school graduates may have many reasons for going, and their parents may have many reasons for supporting them. Either of them may have hidden or unknown motivations, not always in the best interest of the intended student. Sorting out what the primary motivation is can take months of critical examination on the part of all concerned.

In recent years, more and more students are enrolling or reenrolling in college at ages older than the traditional 18 to 22.

In 1994, 62% of college enrolled students were 22 years old and older. Twenty-one percent were 35 and older, a figure that has more than tripled since 1970. [11] This is a good sign, since older students attend for more positive reasons, that is, largely for personal and vocational enhancement. Younger students often attend for negative reasons, that is, for reasons which will not allow them to utilize fully the time, money, and energy invested in their college venture. High school graduates especially, as well as their parents, should, before any application is sent, seriously question what their reasons are. Consider some of the negative reasons for attending college.

Indoctrination.

Some colleges and universities expect their faculties to teach certain systems of thought (social, economic, political, religious, etc.) without too much critical examination. Students who attend such institutions want affirmation of, not challenge to, their already-established knowledge and beliefs, and, to that end, they willingly accept regulations, sometimes in the extreme, of their personal activities and behavior. Most American colleges and universities of this nature represent various fundamental religious groups, but others, subtly if not openly, promote racism, gender discrimination, extreme patriotism, or a combination of all.

Fun and games.

Many students primarily seek the lighter side of college and university life – the athletic events, the beach weekends, or, for that matter, any kind of weekend, the fraternity, sorority, dormitory parties, or any other kind of activity offered as a diversion to the grim and tedious business of study.

Many institutions encourage this party-time image through their promotions and advertisements to prospective students. A typical example of this mentality could be seen a few years ago when a university a few miles from an east-coast beach distributed video packages to recruits which showed students tossing mortarboard caps in the air, waving to cameras, and gleefully motoring away from campus in a red convertible with a surfboard sticking out of the back seat. College alumni associations continue this adolescent behavior by convincing their graduates that college was the best time of their lives and that coming back regularly to party at the Old Alma Mater is a wholesome and worthwhile activity.

However, for fun-and-games students, nothing so sets the tone of higher education as college and university athletics programs. College sports programs must take the larger share of responsibility for the overemphasis of athletics in American high schools discussed in Chapters Two and Three. They have created the illusion that big-time sports are profitable and a necessary ingredient in a good academic program. Except for a handful of institutions, they are not profitable, and they are certainly not a necessary component.

Colleges and universities compete vigorously, sometimes savagely, for the best high school athletes, provide them with free tuition, living expenses, and a four-year training camp for the professional teams. They set standards that plainly favor athletic over educational performance. Unfortunately, it is not likely that higher education can change much of that situation. Presidents and the faculties, especially in the larger universities in Division I of the National Collegiate Athletic Association, have little control over the sports dynasties which exist in their institutions and little political power to withstand the wrath of the alumni, legislators, or trustees should they attempt to make changes.

And yet, if the truth were known, most of them would agree with Wayne Barrett, Associate Editor of *USA Today*, when he said, "Anyone who thinks the U.S government is leading the league in lying and cheating hasn't been following the National Collegiate Athletic Association." [13] And most of them, if they had the nerve, would be happy to rid their campuses of what Clark Kerr, former president of the University of California, once called "the three major administrative problems on a campus: sex for the students, athletics for the alumni, and parking for the faculty." [14]

Colleges and universities cannot, with any measure of integrity, continue to exploit athletics for the recruitment of students or use their campuses and facilities for entertaining the general public, cannot operate professional athletics programs which function under amateur regulations, and cannot allow their coaches, as well as all others associated with big-time collegiate sports, to benefit from lucrative business contracts while paying athletes the paltry wages of room, board, and tuition.

> It has never occurred to a living soul to protect the universities and the students from TV and from the commercialization of both the students and the university . . . But we have allowed TV, which is part of the private sector, in effect, to destroy our undergraduates and harm the universities. To me, that is the true scandal of big time college sports and the American educational system. [12]
>
> —Bart Giamatti, Commissioner of Baseball, 1989, in Howard Cosell, *What's Wrong With Sports*

Leaving home.

Learning to function independently is always, under any circumstance, an important goal for any child. But college is an expensive proposition just to learn to be independent unless there are other, more dominant reasons for going. A child can gain freedom from home much more cheaply and much more efficiently by getting a job, moving out of the house, and paying his or her own bills. Even if children learn to manage their own lives while in college, it should be remembered that, although they may acquire more knowledge, there is not much evidence that the college experience is any better or worse at changing students' attitudes or making them any wiser than any other experience they may choose. One important exception to this is when students deliberately searching for change find a college or university openly willing to help them with that change.

Some children who leave their relatively sheltered homes may be disillusioned to find that the real world can be harsh, cruel, and demanding. Some may make temporary, radical changes in their lifestyles. But most will exert just enough effort to pass, expand their stores of knowledge a little, grow up some, graduate, and leave with their values about the same as when they entered. That is what most parents want. Let the apple fall from the tree, but not too far. Children should rise above their backgrounds and be better than their parents, but not too far above and not too much better.

Average to poor academic performance and
not knowing what else to do.

Every year a large number of students with average to mediocre performance records graduate from high school and go on to college because they don't know what else to do and some college somewhere will take them. Colleges should not take them, but they do, and such students should not enroll, but they do because they don't have much choice. They are the victims of a public school system that in 13 years offered them no alternative to the academic program and dumped them out with little or no employment counseling or training.

The only truly positive reason for attending college is for personal and vocational enhancement. Any other reason demeans the college and its students. Children may legitimately include all of the above negative reasons, and others, in their overall plans for attending college. Indoctrination, having fun, watching athletic events, leaving home, or learning to be independent can be a part of a good college education as long as the serious attempt to improve oneself, personally and vocationally, is the *dominant* motivation. Such motivated children should make definite, personal commitments to college study long before the senior year in high school and should have the performance records and behavior patterns to prove it. If there is any question about that kind of motivation, if high school records are questionable and behavior still unpredictable, if they appear to be aimlessly following friends or a girl or a boy with not much idea about what they want to do, if attending is largely to appease Mom and Dad, then it would be best to delay. They should be encouraged, instead, to gain experience, mature, prove some things to themselves and their parents, grow up more, and learn to support themselves. That is a message parents should convey from kindergarten: we will pay for you to attend college only if your work through elementary and high school has earned you that privilege. Is there a chance they may never go? Yes, but if the motivation is basically there, they will, like the majority who enroll now, go back at a later time for the right reasons.

Colleges in the Northeast and those with fraternities, sororities, and big sports programs are the most likely to attract binge drinkers and turn non-drinking freshmen into alcohol abusers . . . a study from the Harvard School of Public Health shows that certain high risk campuses pose an enormous hazard for non-bingeing freshmen. Forty per cent of them became binge drinkers when exposed to life at a high risk campus . . . survey results showed that one-third of campuses had student bodies in which 50% or more of the students were binge drinkers. At some schools, the figure rose as high as 70%.[15]

— Associated Press Release in the *Rocky Mount* (NC) *Telegram*

In Shakespeare's *Hamlet*, guards are apprehensive about an apparition they have been seeing at night on the castle wall which they think may be the ghost of Hamlet's father. They bring a doubting Horatio, who is a friend of Hamlet's and a well-educated man, to see for himself. When the apparition appears, one of the men turns to Horatio and says, "Thou art a scholar, speak to it . . ." His statement reflects an attitude held sacred by higher education for centuries and one that is losing ground in colleges everywhere in America today: that a formally educated man or woman, a college graduate, as much as humanly possible – especially in a world of technology, its subsequent knowledge explosion, and specialized employment – should know something about many things, including, perhaps, how to talk to ghosts. No parent or nation can expect a more positive reason for children to attend college.

Number 2: Search For the College
That Fits the Reasons For Attending.

It is a relatively easy task to find appropriate colleges for those students who attend for the negative reasons discussed above. Parents or children who want established beliefs confirmed, who want an education that does not in any way challenge their own ideas, should find the least expensive accredited college that imparts their own prejudices and accept, from the beginning, that the diploma awarded will be considered inferior.

It is possible for fun-and-games students to pick up a little education on the side while enrolled in a college. Most, however, if they do manage to graduate and not drop out or flunk out, will share three common characteristics: they had a good time, they did not get a very good education, and they wasted a lot of somebody's money. Parents with these kinds of children should find the least expensive accredited college possible that has large and intensely competitive athletic programs and a less than rigorous academic program. These kinds of students, prone to rowdy, party-animal behavior, will always find each other. The parents' best hope is that their children will learn something more from their experiences than how not to approach college studies.

As for learning to be independent, parents should be grateful to children who want to escape from home rule and learn to function on their own, but parents should also help them discover another, more positive reason for attending college. Find an inexpensive accredited college, preferably at least 300 miles from home. Make sure the changes from the home environment to the college environment are not too severe, turn them loose, and pray they don't spend too much more money learning to be independent than they would in getting a job and moving out of the house.

For those students with average to mediocre performances in high school and not much interest in anything, the only option they or their parents have is to play the game. Search for the easiest, least expensive accredited college and hope the academic program is lax enough to graduate them.

It is more complicated to find the right college for children who are attending primarily for personal or vocational enhancement and have proved by their performances that they have the emotional and intellectual maturity to profit from college study. For them and their parents, such a search should be taken seriously. Some already know what they want in a career and some are uncertain. In both cases, they should be encouraged to search for colleges which require an exposure to a wide variety of subjects, which demand high levels of performance from students, and which are affordable.

Considerable time should be spent studying the many publications that offer information about colleges and universities. Public and high school libraries and school counselors will have a wealth of information. Consider any college, near or far, that has a quality program, regardless of expense, whether you know about it or never heard of it. At this point, you are looking for the best college for the child's purpose. When publications, catalogs, or brochures, fail to answer appropriate questions, have the child write the institutions involved asking whatever questions are necessary. Personalize the inquiries. Give information about test scores, grades, interest, and activities participated in. Let them know the child is interested and that enrollment there will be dependent on what kind of answers they send and how much help they can give.

Eventually, your search process should narrow the field to a select few colleges or universities which appear to have the programs with the quality you want. These are the ones you and your child will want to visit. The number is limited only by how much time and money you can afford. If you have 10 institutions on the list and can afford the visits, by all means do so. It is critical that a child visit a college which he or she may attend. Arrange with the admissions offices for a tour of the campus, and at least one, but preferably both parents should go. Also request, on the same day, an appointment with the dean or the highest academic official possible. (Most are men, but it could be a woman.)

The degree of difficulty in getting to this person will tell you something about the college's commitment to helping a student find the right fit. As a rule, the larger the college, the greater the difficulty. Persist. Let the child go with the recruiters to tour the landmarks, the football or soccer fields, the dorms, and the student activity centers. Parents should see the dean. College administrators prefer that you talk to the recruiters from the admissions office because they are closer to your child's age and will tend to talk about how much fun there is at their college. The dean won't like talking to you, either, because he doesn't like to think of himself as *in loco parentis*, that is, as taking the place of the parents. He is likely to think: "Why won't these people turn their kid loose? Do they think I will tuck him in at night? I don't have the time to talk to students *and* faculty *and* parents. If there is a question, let the kid come to see me."

And parents won't say it, but they will think it: "We'll turn the kid loose. You better believe we'll turn her loose. We can't wait for her to make her own decisions and pay her own bills. And we don't want you to take our place. You *will* be, whether you like it or not, only, we suspect, with a lot less care and much less supervision and control. Right now she is an 18-year-old greenhorn who thinks she knows everything, but, when you come down to it, she barely knows how to get in out of the rain.

You will deliberately expose her to a number of good and bad influences and dangerous, sometimes harebrained, ideas, and we will pay the freight for it all. The very least you can do is try not to make me feel stupid for asking how you plan to do all of this."

You will want to ask the dean four questions. He should know the answers. If he squirms and refuses to give them to you straight, it means one of three things: 1) he knows the answers and won't tell you; 2) he doesn't know the answers and doesn't want you to know it; or, 3) he doesn't care one way or the other. If you detect any of these, terminate the conversation, wait for your child to come back from the expensive slide show about the college, and look elsewhere.

If the dean knows the answers, is forthright in discussing them, and doesn't hesitate to explain why they do what they do, apologizes maybe for things he hopes to improve, then you might be in a good college even if you don't like what you are told.

It is important, however, to consider the answers to those four fundamental questions about the quality of their instructional program.

Do senior professors teach freshman classes,
and can professors be tenured on the basis of teaching performance?

This will tell you what their commitment is to teaching. At too many colleges, part-time or junior instructors teach "in the pits," in the beginning courses, so that the more experienced and knowledgeable professors can teach their specialties to advanced students or work on their research projects. The junior instructors may be good teachers, better even than the full professors. That isn't the point. If senior professors don't teach freshmen, and if junior professors cannot be promoted for their teaching skills, it's because the college's general attitude is that research, publication, and scholarship are more important than teaching.

What is the academic profile of your student body?

The quality of education at a college is dependent on three critical factors of equal importance: the scholarship and teaching competence of the faculty, the intelligence and motivation of the students, and the extent to which the college is willing to apply rigor and discipline to its instructional program. What would be the point in sending a child to a college where the student body is not much better than the local beer joint cowboys, or no different from the crowd he usually runs with?

What percentage of students who
apply for admission are rejected?

Many colleges, like the public schools, labor with the burden of having to take anyone who comes to them, and they will be forever limited because of it. What is the point in sending a child to college for challenge and growth when anybody with a pulse can get in?

When a student doesn't perform well, how long is he
allowed to remain enrolled and under what conditions?

There isn't any effective way for a college to discipline a student except by probation and suspension. Probation, either social or academic, is an alert that, unless conditions change, the student will be suspended. Suspension is the capital punishment of higher education: separation, sometimes temporary, sometimes permanent, from the college community. It is the only way a college keeps its programs clean and respectable. "Grow up," it says. "Get serious. We don't want you when you don't perform and unless you change, you are out of here." Colleges reluctant to suspend a student care more about a loss of tuition and less about their integrity.

> It is one of the most obvious weaknesses of our American universities that they have done such a poor job of convincing the young that learning, that things of the mind, are enjoyable. Here you have these great institutions of higher learning with their well-endowed libraries and laboratories — institutions that are the envy of the world — yet somehow the majority of students are not really drawn to them. They gather, for the most part, outside the walls, flitting about and enjoying themselves according to their own tastes. [16]
>
> —George H. Douglas in *Education Without Impact*

If any one of these questions is not answered to your satisfaction, keep looking.

Number 3: Selection of the Best College With the Best Price.

By this time parents and child have visited selected colleges and made judgments about the best-liked ones. Now comes crunch time when money becomes an important factor in the final decision. Your slogan should be "Use Somebody Else's Money to Send My Child to College." (See Appendices G and H for average costs of public and private colleges by state.) The better your child's performance in high school, the higher the SAT scores, the more the participation and leadership in student activities, or the greater the athletic skills, the more chips parents will have to bargain with a college. You should do it with fervor and without shame, and at no time should you feel sorry for them, else you won't strike a hard enough bargain. In the past 30 years, colleges have soaked the American public with expensive charges. Undergraduate college tuition and fees, not including room and board, have increased by 558% in public institutions and 802% in private institutions, [17] and they have not been able to explain adequately, during many of those years, why these charges were higher than inflation rates. There are thousands of sources of aid for college students in the form of scholarships, grants, loans, and work options. What they are and how to get at them are in public, high school, and counselor libraries. In addition, the colleges will have their own stock of scholarship, grant, and loan funds, and many of the loans are with low interest. Don't be afraid or ashamed to ask about any of them. Scholarships and grants are preferable. Take out loans only when you have exhausted all other sources.

Here are some suggestions that might also be of help.

Percentage of change in real dollars, since 1984, in average tuition:
at a private college: +47
at a public college: +60[18]
Harper's Magazine "Index"

Think about this one if you have a child you suspect is attending college for negative reasons or is one of those with a poor high school record.

There are aboriginal tribes that require an adolescent man to participate in a "walkabout." When he reaches a certain age, his parents give him a three-day supply of food and tell him, literally, to leave, visit other places, meet other people, and learn to take care of himself. By this method, he must prove his maturity before he can come home and take his place as a responsible citizen of the community.

Why not delay college a couple of years, for male or female children, and put them to work earning their own money and being responsible, as much as possible, for making their own way? Let them move out or not, but if they stay at home, it should be with the understanding that they will continue to live by the family rules, pay something for room and board, and set something aside from each paycheck for future college expenses. Tell them you and the rest of the family will work hard to help all you can, but the burden must fall largely with him or her.

You say there aren't many suitable jobs out there for a high school graduate with no experience? You're right, and that is the point. He soon learns that the good jobs with better benefits and salaries go to those with better education. When he has to help pay his own way, he learns more quickly to get his money's worth. A friend of mine put his children on earned allowances and required them to spend their own money for incidentals. During a movie, one of them went to buy a bag of popcorn, but came back without it, complaining about the price. Said my friend, "Do you think he worried about the price of popcorn when I was paying for it?"

Use family members wherever possible.

Is there a family member willing to supply room and board near one of the selected colleges? Or is there a grandfather willing to provide an interest-free loan?

Consider the possibility of having the student live at home and attend a local community college with a two-year general education program, but only if the credits can be transferred to a senior college.

Some of these colleges have excellent programs, and their low tuition could save a bundle, including room and board savings.

Don't forget about the non-collegiate post-secondary schools which are legitimate and train people in all sorts of good, highly employable skills.

There are directories of these schools in the libraries, for example, *Peterson's Guide to Vocational and Technical Schools.*

Consider the military.

Appointments to the military academies are for a highly select group who must also be politically appointed. But ROTC is available in many high schools, and the regular military branches are very cooperative, where possible and appropriate, about paying for college, if long-term commitments are made. Even if they are not interested in attending college, military personnel get paid while learning skills that can be used outside the military.

Athletes and Smaller colleges.

Many smaller colleges will work very hard to provide scholarships or work-study assistance for students who are good athletes but not good enough to play in larger colleges.

AFTERWORD

Thank you for reading this book.

You are right if you think the chapters and the book itself end abruptly. I tried to do it that way, tried diligently to make my point quickly, explain it briefly, stop, and go on to the next. I have done everything I know to make this an interesting and challenging book. I wanted it to be readable, that is, short, simple, and to the point. I failed in these objectives if you skipped pages or kept laying it aside for another time.

You are right if you concluded that politicians, professional educators, or students cannot change our educational system. Who, then, can? Who else but parents and grandparents?

You are right if you think I have proposed only brief guidelines. No individual, no matter how learned or visionary, can alone prescribe what our schools should be. That requires a national effort by many people and many groups. For all practical purposes, this book is a primer, a book of fundamental principles, and its main premise, from its inception to its completion, has been that we cannot reform American education until we take the six steps I have proposed. If I were King of America, I would issue a decree that all schools and colleges immediately implement them. Then, and only then, would I think about the details.

You are wrong if you think I am the voice of a radical. Yes, there are a number of things I would change overnight, if possible, about America. But the principles behind those six steps represent American values as traditional and conservative as apple pie and ice cream. Successful individuals, families, and businesses live by them daily.

You are wrong if you think my ideas are set in granite. They are the results of a lifetime of experience with four children, 10 grandchildren, thousands of students, and dozens of schools and colleges. But they are subject to change. Do you like my ideas? Do you have better ones? I would like to hear them. Do you want me to speak to a local group? Would you like to hold a seminar? I can arrange it. Or, do you just want to get some things off your chest? Write me in care of Rainbow Books, Inc., Highland City, Florida, 33846-0430, or if you are on the Internet, send me Email at either simschul@coastalnet.com or to my publisher at NAIP@aol.com.

Maybe together we can figure out a way to stimulate more interest in better ways to educate our children.

Endnotes

Chapter 1

[1] U.S. Department of Education, *Digest of Education Statistics 1996* (Washington, DC: U.S. Government Printing Office, 1996), Table 38, p. 50.

[2] Ibid., Table 5, p. 14.

[3] From a letter to Colonel Charles Yancey, January 18, 1816.

[4] Calvin H. Wiley, *The North Carolina Reader Number III* (New York: A.S. Barnes and Burr, 1855), p. 6.

[5] Lawrence A. Cremin, *The Genius of American Education* (New York: Vintage Books, 1965), p. 35.

[6] *Digest of Education Statistics 1996*, Table 3, p. 12.

[7] The Commission on Skills of the American Workforce, *America's Choice: High Skills or Low Wages* (Rochester, New York:

National Center on Education and the Economy, 1990), p. 45.

[8] Margaret Mead, *Culture and Commitment* (New York: Doubleday and Company, 1970), pp. 87-88.

[9] *Digest of Education Statistics 1996,* Table 3, p. 12, and Table 5, p. 14.

[10] (Pierce vs. Society of Sisters) 268 U.S. 510 45 S.Ct. 571 69 L. Ed. 1070 (1925).

[11] Benjamin R. Barber, "America Skips School." *Harper's Magazine* Vol. 287, No. 1722 (November, 1993): p. 45.

[12] See Appendix A.

[13] See Appendix B.

[14] *Digest of Education Statistics 1996,* Table 6, p. 15.

[15] Ibid., Table 32, p. 36.

[16] Ibid., Table 33, p. 37.

[17] Using the 1995 Bureau of Census estimate of the United States population, Table 2, p. 8, *Statistical Abstract of the United States, 1996,* and the 66,996,000 enrolled students listed in Appendix B of this book.

[18] The national debt on February 27, 1997 at 8:53:21 AM PST, according to the U.S. National Debt Clock, (www.brillig.com), was $5,345,481,619,301.73. (Divide by the total amount of expenditures

shown in Appendix D.)

[19] Field Report from Kaolack, Senegal Field Office, PLAN International, Childreach, 155 Plan Way, Warwick, R.I., Summer, 1995.

CHAPTER 2

[1] Margaret Mead, *Culture and Commitment* (New York: Doubleday and Company, 1970), pp. 87-88.

[2] Mary Fran Spencer, retired teacher of 30 years, "Retrain Teachers? Let's Retrain Society Instead," Raleigh (N.C.) *The News and Observer* (May 30, 1993), p. 25A.

[3] *U.S. Bureau of Census: Statistical Abstract of the United States* (Washington, DC, 1996): p.1.

[4] Mary Cooper, "Infant Mortality," *CQ Researcher* Vol. 2, No. 28 (July 31, 1992): p. 644.

[5] Charles S. Clark, "Child Sexual Abuse," *CQ Researcher* Vol. 3, No. 2 (January 15, 1993): pp. 33 and 39.

[6] Richard S. Worsnop, "Teenage Suicide," *CQ Researcher* Vol. 1, No. 6 (June 14, 1991): pp. 373-374 and 376.

[7] Sarah Glazer, "Preventing Teen Pregnancy," *CQ Researcher* Vol. 3, No. 18 (May 14, 1993): p. 415.

[8] Robert Famighetti, Editor, *The World Almanac* (Mahwah,

N.J.: Funk and Wagnalls, 1994), p. 957.

[9] *The American Almanac* , 1993-94, Table 91, p. 73.

[10] Susan Kellam, "Child Custody and Support," *CQ Researcher* Vol. 5, No. 2 (January 13, 1995): p. 28.

[11] *The American Almanac, 1993-94* Table 737, p. 470.

[12] Ibid., p. 389.

[13] Age Wave Institute, Emeryville, CA and Population Reference Bureau, Washington, D.C. both quoted in *The Washington Spectator* Vol. 19, No. 19 (November 15, 1993): pp. 1 and 3.

[14] Jonathan Kozol, *Savage Inequalities* (New York: Crown Publishers, Incorporated, 1991), Chapter 3.

[15] U.S. Department of Education, *Digest of Education Statistics 1996* (Washington, DC: U.S. Government Printing Office, 1996), Table 32, p. 36.

[16] Jonathan Walters, "School Funding," *CQ Researcher* Vol. 3, No. 32 (August 27, 1993): p. 748.

[17] Kathleen O'Leary Morgan, et. al., Editor, *State Rankings 1993* (Lawrence, Kansas: Morgan Quitno Corporation, 1993), pp. 117-129.

[18] Jonathan Walters, "School Funding," *CQ Researcher* Vol. 3, No. 32 (August 27, 1993): p. 750.

[19] Paul Gagnon, "What Should Children Learn?" *The Atlantic Monthly* Vol. 276, No. 6 (December, 1995): p. 67.

[20] Randy Roberts and James S. Olson, *Winning Is the Only Thing* (Baltimore: The Johns Hopkins University Press, 1989), p. 234.

[21] From an Associated Press news release published on the first page of the sports section in the Raleigh (NC) *News and Observer*, November 27, 1995.

[22] *Digest of Education Statistics* 1996, Table 149, p. 142.

[23] Public and private high school enrollment, grades 9-12, and the number of high schools are taken from the *Digest of Education Statistics 1996*, Table 3, p. 12 and table 5, p. 14. Athletic participation in the 10 most popular high school sports for 1993-94 is taken from the *1994-1995 Handbook*, National Federation of State High School Associations, Kansas City, Missouri.

Estimates of figures quoted were determined by the following methods: the number of athletes listed by the National Federation is 5,283,841, but that figure is the number of participations and includes students who may play more than one sport. Assume that one-third are duplications and subtract from the total. That leaves 3,522,561.

Further assume that an additional 10% are not represented in National Federation figures because their schools are not members. Subtract them. That leaves 3,170,305.

Assume that 90% of this last figure will function adequately as students. That leaves 317,030 (2.33% of total enrollment) (14.4 per school nationally) who might not function adequately as students and who *might* remain in school because of athletics.

[24] Robin Brinkley and Harry Minium, "Virginia Police Probe Possible Prep Fixing" quoted in The Raleigh (NC) *News and Observer*, March 7, 1996.

[25] Robert Sinclair and Ward J. Ghory, *Reaching Marginal Students: A Primary Concern for School Renewal* (Berkeley, CA: McCutchan Publishing Corporation, 1987), p. 14.

[26] (Wisconsin vs. Yoder) 406 U.S. 205 92 S. Ct. 1526 32 L.Ed. 2d 15 (1972).

[27] Everett Reimer, *School Is Dead* (Garden City, N.Y.: Doubleday and Company, Incorporated, 1971), p. 176.

Chapter 3

[1] Harold Hodgkinson, "American Education: The Good, the Bad and the Task," *Phi Delta Kappan* Vol. 74, No. 8 (April, 1993): pp. 619-623.

[2] John Herbers, "Local Government Needs Reinventing, Too," *The Washington Spectator* Vol. 19, No. 20 (November 1, 1993): p. 1.

[3] John E. Chubb and Terry Moe, *Politics, Markets, and America's Schools* (Washington, D.C.: The Brookings Institution, 1990), p. 68.

[4] Educational Policies Commission, *School Athletics: Problems*

and Policies. Washington, DC, National Education Association, 1954.

[5] Ryan Whirty from a sports news story in *The Rocky Mount* (NC) *Telegram,* November 21, 1995.

[6] John Hoerr, "Commentary," *Business Week* No. 3168 (July 9, 1990): p. 45.

[7] Lawrence A. Cremin, *Popular Education and Its Discontents* (New York: Harper and Row, 1990), p. 29.

[8] John Holt, *The Underachieving School* (New York: Pitman Publishing Corporation, 1969), pp. 28-29.

[9] Chester A. Finn, *We Must Take Charge: Our Schools and Our Future* (New York: The Free Press, 1991), pp. 303-304.

CHAPTER 4

[1] Alan Ehrenhalt, "Learning From the Fifties," *The Wilson Quarterly* Vol. XIX, No. 3 (Summer, 1995): p. 29.

[2] John Rosemond, "The Best Parents Take Their Stand," from a column in the Raleigh (NC) *The News and Observer,* December 19, 1995.

[3] Neil Postman and Charles Weingartner, *Teaching As a Subversive Activity* (New York: Delacorte Press, 1969), p. 41.

[4] From *Who Will Teach Our Children?*, a brochure, Public

School Forum of NC, 3739 National Drive, Raleigh, NC, 27612, no date.

CHAPTER 5

[1] U.S. Department of Education, *Digest of Education Statistics 1996* (Washington, DC: U.S. Government Printing Office, 1996), Table 5, p. 14.

[2] Ibid., Table 5, p. 14.

[3] Ibid., Table 5, p. 14.

[4] Ibid., Table 167, p. 174.

[5] Ibid., Table 5, p. 14, and Table 3, p. 12.

[6] Ibid., Table 210, p. 216.

[7] Nicholas LeMann, "Making It, Pt. 2," (A review of *Getting In: Inside the College Admissions Process* by Bill Paul.) (Reading, Maine, Addison-Wesley, 1995) in *The Washington Monthly* Vol. 28, No. 3 (March, 1996): p. 48.

[8] *Digest of Education Statistics 1996,* Table 5, p. 14, and Table 167, p. 174.

[9] Ibid., Table 309, pp. 320-321.

[10] Michele N-K Collison, "As Students Cram Rooms With Electronic Gadgetry, Colleges Scramble to Meet the Demand

for Power," excerpted from *The Chronicle of Higher Education* Vol. XXXVIII (September 25, 1991): pp. A1 and A42.

[11] *Digest of Education Statistics 1996*, Table 171, p. 178.

[12] Bart Giamatti quoted in Howard Cosell, *What's Wrong With Sports* (New York: Simon and Schuster, 1991), p. 37.

[13] Wayne M. Barret, "Curb Campus Corruption," *USA Today* Vol. 118, No. 2540 (May, 1990): p. 93.

[14] Clark Kerr, *Time Magazine* Vol. LXXII, No. 20 (November 17, 1958): p. 96.

[15] Associated Press release in *The Rocky Mount* (NC) *Telegram*, November 2, 1995.

[16] George H. Douglas, *Education Without Impact* (New York, Birch Lane Press, 1992), pp. 169-170.

[17] *Digest of Education Statistics 1996*, Table 309, pp. 320-321.

[18] "Index," *Harper Magazine* Vol. 291, No. 1744 (September, 1995): p. 9.

OTHER

[1] Appendix I: The Ten Most Popular High School Sports, 1993-94, from the *National Federation Handbook, 1994-95* of the National Federation of State High School Associations, Kansas City, Missouri.

Suggested Reading

Books

John E. Chubb and Terry Moe, *Politics, Markets, and America's Schools*. Washington, DC, The Brookings Institution, 1990.

Howard Cosell, *What's Wrong With Sports*. New York, Simon and Schuster, 1991.

Lawrence A. Cremin, *The Genius of American Education*. New York, Vintage Books, 1965.

George H. Douglas, *Education Without Impact*. New York, Birch Lane Press, 1992.

Chester A. Finn, *We Must Take Charge: Our Schools and Our Future*. New York, The Free Press, 1991.

Jonathan Kozol, *Savage Inequalities*. New York, Crown Publishers, Incorporated, 1991.

Randy Roberts and James S. Olson, *Winning Is the Only Thing.* Baltimore, The Johns Hopkins University Press, 1989.

John Rosemond, *A Family of Value.* Kansas City, Andrews and McMeel, a Universal Press Syndicate Company, 1996.

MAGAZINE ARTICLES

Benjamin R. Barber, "America Skips School." *Harper's Magazine* Vol. 287, No. 1722 (November, 1993): p. 45.

Paul Gagnon, "What Should Children Learn?" *The Atlantic Monthly* Vol. 276, No. 6 (December, 1995): p. 67.

Harold Hodgkinson, "American Education: The Good, the Bad, and the Task," *Phi Delta Kappan* Vol. 74, No. 8 (April, 1993): p. 619.

Introduction to the Appendices

Attempts to count the agencies, people, and money involved in American education on any given day or year are like trying to count how many dollars are in the national debt or how many people work in the federal bureaucracy. The figures change every minute. Now you see them, now you don't, and they won't sit still while you count.

The numbers in the tables that follow are conservative. That is, there are more educational institutions in this country, more people involved, and more money spent than listed because there is no reliable, systematic way to gather much of the data needed. There is a good count on the numbers of people involved in regular or traditional education such as schools and colleges, thanks to the enduring work of the staff of the National Center for Educational Statistics. But there is not a good count on those who take continuing education programs, self-improvement courses, courses for the fun of it, or those who participate in business and corporate training programs.

The American Society for Training and Development, for example, has a staff of 120, a $15 million budget, and 55,000 members, most of whom are training officers and consultants for in-house business and corporate programs. It is only one of the 1,300 organizations, from the two-million-member National Education Association to the 85-member American Association of Teachers of Turkish, that is associated with some aspect of education, but rarely do their students, employees, or expenditures show up in any statistical count. Also not listed are businesses producing or largely selling school supplies or the numerous political, social, and religious groups whose main functions are educational.

We know fairly well how many non-collegiate vocational schools there are, and we have a rational means for making an estimate of their employees, but we have no clear picture of how much money they spend. We know the number of those 1,300 educational support groups because we can count them in the *Encyclopedia of Associations*, but their staff members and expenditures are not so clear.

Even when sources are reliable and collection methods valid, there are still problems in consolidating the data into one table. Some of it may be based on sample surveys and some on estimates. Two sets of data may not be comparable from one year to the next or even in the same year, and sometimes, figures for a previous year are revised. For some groups the tables will report part-time and full-time head count on employees, and some will report FTE or full time equivalents.

However, acknowledging these limitations, it is possible to add up the numbers available from reliable sources that use systematic methods of collection, and, with assistance from a variety of groups, estimate the rest. What you will read in the following tables may have some missing figures, and there may have been over – or under – estimations of others, but the numbers are essentially there. Their purpose is to give the reader a feel for the magnitude of American education, not to get statistically accurate numbers.

Appendix A

Estimated Number
of Educational Institutions in America

State Departments of Public Instruction – 50

Public School Districts (94-95) – 14,772

Public Elementary and Secondary Schools (93-94) – 85,393

Private Elementary and Secondary Schools (93-94) – 26,093

Public Non-Collegiate Institutions (93-94) – 527

Private Non-Collegiate Institutions (Non-Profit)(93-94) – 1,203

Proprietary Non-Collegiate Institutions (93-94) – 5,007

Public Colleges and Universities (93-94) – 1,625

Private Colleges and Universities (Non-Profit) (93-94) – 1,687

Proprietary Colleges and Universities (93-94) – 320

Boards of Directors for Pvt.Elem. and Sec. Schools – *26,093

Boards of Trustees for Public/Pvt. Colleges/Univ. – *3,312

Educational Organizations and Associations – *1,294

Federal Government Department of Education – 1

Total – 167,377

* Estimates. All figures except the estimates are from the *Digest of Education Statistics 1996*, Tables 5 and 88, pages 14 and 96.

Appendix B

Estimated Number of People Involved in American Education

Public School Elem. and Sec. Enrollment (1997) – 46,524,000

Private School Elem. and Sec. Enrollment (1997) – 5,876,000

Public School Teachers and Staff (1994) – 4,907,996

Private School Teachers and Staff – *534,636

Local Public School Board Members – *97,000

State Boards of Education Members – *600

State Departments of Education Staff – *30,900

Public College Enrollment (1997) – 11,405,000

Private College Enrollment (1997) – 3,191,000

Public College Faculty and Staff (1993-94) – 1,812,513

Private College Faculty and Staff (1993-94) – 790,099

Public College Trustees — *17,712

Private College Trustees — *50,779

Adult Basic and Secondary Education Enrollment (1991)–
3,694,217

Federal Department of Education Staff — *6,000

Public Non-Collegiate Post-Secondary Enrollment (1993-94) –
314,924

Private Non-Collegiate Post-Secondary Enrollment (1993-94) –
566,712

Public Non-Collegiate Post-Secondary Faculty and Staff (1993)–
31,554

Private Non-College Post-Secondary Faculty and Staff — 93,338

Total — 79,944,980

*Estimates. All figures except the estimates are from the *Digest of Education Statistics, 1996:* Table 2, p. 11, Table 81, p. 89, Table 59, p. 71, Table 167, p. 174, and Table 352, p. 364.

Appendix C

Selected Organizations and Associations Related to Education

Listed in the *Encyclopedia of Assocations* (1993)
Section 5 - "Education"

Organizations	Members	Budget	Staff
Nat.Cong.Par.& Teach.	7,000,000	Not Reported	70
Nat. Education Assoc.	2,000,800	$147,500,000	600
Am. Fed. of Teachers	780,000	40,000,000	600
Assn./Super.& Curr.Dev.	150,000	14,000,000	124
Nat.Counc.Teach.of Eng.	120,000	Not Reported	80
Inter. Reading Assoc.	93,000	6,707,555	80
Nat.Assoc.Ed.Young Child	75,000	5,000,000	45
Am.Soc./Train.& Dev.	55,000	15,000,000	120
Assoc./Sec.Sch.Princ.	43,000	18,500,000	90

Organizations	Members	Budget	Staff
Am. Assoc./Univ. Prof.	42,000	3,073,000	34
Modern Lang.Assoc./Am.	30,000	5,000,000	88
Nat.Catholic Ed.Assoc.	20,000	3,000,000	45
Am.Assoc./Sch.Administr.	19,000	9,000,000	65
Am.Fed./Sch.Administr.	12,000	600,000	6
Council for Basic Ed.	4,000	2,500,000	12
Am.Assoc./Cont. Ed.	4,000	500,000	8
The College Board	2,800	Not Reported	325
Assoc./State Bds./Ed.	590	2,000,000	18
Am.Assoc/Christ.Schools	250	300,000	7
Am.Assoc./Bible Colleges	107	300,000	5
Am.Assoc./Teach. of Turkish	85	25,000	NR

Appendix D

Estimated Total Expenditures for Private and Public Educational Institutions by Source of Funds

1993-1994
(in billions of dollars)

Source of Funds	Elem./Sec.	Higher Ed.	Total
Federal	18.7	23.6	42.3
State	119.8	44.8	164.6
Local	119.7	5.3	125.0
All Other	29.3	117.9	147.2
Totals	287.5	191.6	479.1

Read the Grand Total as: $479,100,000,000
(479 Billion, One Hundred Million Dollars)

From the *Digest of Education Statistics 1996,* Table 32, page 36.

APPENDIX E

ESTIMATED PERCENTAGES OF SOURCES OF FUNDS FOR EXPENDITURES BY ALL AMERICAN EDUCATIONAL INSTITUTIONS 1992-1993

SOURCE	PUBLIC	PRIVATE
Elementary and Secondary Education		
Federal	7.0	–
State	45.2	–
Local	45.1	–
All Other	2.7	100.0
Institutions of Higher Education		
Federal	11.0	14.5
State	35.9	2.1
Local	4.0	0.7
All Other	49.1	82.7

SOURCE	PUBLIC	PRIVATE
Total for Elementary, Scondary, Higher Education		
Federal	8.3	11.0
State	42.3	1.6
Local	32.3	0.6
All Other	17.2	86.7

From the *Digest of Education Statistics 1996*, Table 32, p. 36.

APPENDIX F

CURRENT FUND REVENUE OF PUBLIC AND PRIVATE INSTITUTIONS OF HIGHER EDUCATION BY SOURCE, 1993-1994

SOURCE	PUBLIC	PRIVATE
Tuition and Fees	18.4%	42.0%
State Government	35.9%	2.1%
Local Government	4.0%	0.7%
Sales and Services	23.4%	23.2%
Private Gifts	4.0%	8.6%
Federal Grants/Contracts	11.0%	14.5%
Endowed Income	0.6%	4.6%
Other	2.7%	4.3%

From the *Digest of Education Statistics 1996*, Tables 322 and 323, pages 334 and 335.

Appendix G

Average Undergraduate Tuition, Fees, Room, and Board by State at Four-Year *Public* Institutions of Higher Education for One Year, 1994-1995

National Average = $6,674

Rank	State	Cost
1.	Vermont	$10,401
2.	Rhode Island	9,080
3.	New Jersey	8,714
4.	Pennsylvania	8,665
5.	Massachusetts	8,536
6.	Connecticut	8,505
7.	Maryland	8,297
8.	New Hampshire	8,145
9.	Delaware	8,131
10.	New York	7,952
11.	Virginia	7,951
12.	Michigan	7,949
13.	California	7,922
14.	Maine	7,794
15.	Ohio	7,733
16.	Illinois	7,482

Rank	State	Cost
17.	Washington	7,070
18.	Oregon	6,929
19.	Indiana	6,921
20.	Nevada	6,908
21.	South Carolina	6,758
22.	Colorado	6,523
23.	Missouri	6,326
24.	Florida	6,192
25.	Minnesota	6,182
26.	Alaska	6,156
27.	Montana	5,996
28.	West Virginia	5,912
29.	Arizona	5,829
30.	Iowa	5,699
31.	Wisconsin	5,615
32.	North Dakota	5,513
33.	Kansas	5,442
34.	Alabama	5,432
35.	Georgia	5,381
36.	New Mexico	5,373
37.	Utah	5,349
38.	Kentucky	5,324
39.	South Dakota	5,319
40.	Louisiana	5,275
41.	Mississippi	5,248
42.	Wyoming	5,237
43.	Idaho	5,205
44.	Nebraska	5,186
45.	Texas	5,175
46.	Tennessee	5,130

RANK	STATE	COST
47.	Arkansas	4,926
48.	North Carolina	4,858
49.	Oklahoma	4,205
50.	Hawaii	NA

From the *Digest of Education Statistics 1995*, Table 307, p. 319.

APPENDIX H

AVERAGE UNDERGRADUATE TUITION, FEES, ROOM, AND BOARD BY STATE AT FOUR-YEAR *PRIVATE* INSTITUTIONS OF HIGHER EDUCATION FOR ONE YEAR, 1994-1995

National Average = $16,645

RANK	STATE	COST
1.	Massachusetts	$22,322
2.	Connecticut	21,923
3.	Maine	20,853
4.	Rhode Island	20,799
5.	Vermont	20,675
6.	Maryland	20,053
7.	New York	19,481
8.	Pennsylvania	19,035
9.	New Jersey	18,983
10.	California	18,631
11.	Oregon	17,577
12.	New Hampshire	17,162
13.	Washington	16,996
14.	Colorado	16,908
15.	Louisiana	16,764
16.	Minnesota	16,348

Rank	State	Cost
17.	Ohio	16,334
18.	New Mexico	16,004
19.	Illinois	15,986
20.	Indiana	15,923
21.	Iowa	15,274
22.	Wisconsin	14,766
23.	Idaho	14,583
24.	North Carolina	14,544
25.	Virginia	14,519
26.	Florida	14,480
27.	Georgia	14,369
28.	Missouri	14,069
29.	West Virginia	13,835
30.	Tennessee	13,176
31.	Michigan	12,815
32.	South Carolina	12,709
33.	Nebraska	12,573
34.	Alaska	12,448
35.	Texas	12,417
36.	South Dakota	12,385
37.	Oklahoma	11,859
38.	Kansas	11,736
39.	Delaware	11,356
40.	Alabama	11,321
41.	Hawaii	11,000
42.	Kentucky	10,665
43.	Montana	10,406
44.	Arizona	10,179
45.	Arkansas	9,577
46.	North Dakota	9,505

RANK	STATE	COST
47.	Mississippi	9,179
48.	Utah	7,112
49.	Nevada	NA
50.	Wyoming	NA

From the *Digest of Education Statistics 1995*, Table 307, p. 319.

Appendix I

The 10 Most Popular High School Sports 1993-1994

Boys		Girls	
Football	928,134	Basketball	412,576
Basketball	530,068	Track/Field	345,700
Baseball	438,846	Volleyball	327,616
Track/Field	419,758	Softball (Fast)	257,118
Soccer	255,538	Soccer	166,173
Wrestling	233,433	Tennis	136,239
Cross Country	162,188	Cross Country	124,700
Tennis	135,702	Swimming/Diving	102,652
Golf	131,207	Field Hockey	53,747
Swim./Diving	81,328	Softball (Slow)	41,118

From *1994-1995 Handbook,* National Federation of State High School Associations, 1994.

ABOUT THE AUTHOR
SIM O. WILDE, ED.D

Sim Wilde was born and reared near Asheville in the mountains of North Carolina to a school principal father and a homemaker mother.

He graduated from Mars Hill Junior College, Appalachian State University (when it was Appalachian State Teachers' College), Western Carolina University (MA), and the University of North Carolina, Chapel Hill (Ed.D.).

He was a teacher and administrator in the Buncombe County and Asheville City schools for 10 years, earning his masters degree at nights and on weekends. He moved his family to Chapel Hill where he earned his doctorate from UNC and served as Director of the UNC Evening College.

He moved to North Carolina Wesleyan College in Rocky Mount where, over a 17-year period, he was Dean of Students, Professor of Education, and Academic Dean. While at Wesleyan, he was given two awards for outstanding teaching, and he was Chairman of the Human Relations Commission for Rocky Mount when it was named an outstanding commission in North Carolina by Governor James Hunt.

Sim has written articles and book reviews in national and

international journals, digests and newspapers, and has published a novel, *Snyder's Letters.*

He is married with four daughters, two stepdaughters, four sons-in-law, and 10 grandchildren. He is a golfer, a bird watcher, an amateur actor in community theatre, and a yard man for his gardening wife.